REVIVING
the SOUL *of*
TEACHING

We dedicate this book to those teachers

who came before us and made us who we are . . .

Lydia Studebaker Deal

1884–1942

John E. Deal   *Agnes Deal Click*

1904–1991   *1906–1968*

Gerald Vivian Deal   *Marguerite Deal Davisson*   *Robert Louis Deal*

1910–1963   *1912–1967*   *1916–2003*

Joseph Irvin Deal   *Norma Deal Fillmore*

1920–   *1922–*

. . . and to the generations who carry on the Deal family tradition

of teaching.

Terrence E. Deal ▪ Peggy Deal Redman
Foreword by Leonard O. Pellicer

REVIVING *the* SOUL *of* TEACHING

Balancing Metrics and Magic

A Joint Publication

For information:

Corwin Press, Inc.
A SAGE Company
2455 Teller Road
Thousand Oaks, California 91320
www.corwinpress.com

SAGE India Pvt. Ltd.
B 1/I 1 Mohan Cooperative
 Industrial Area
Mathura Road, New Delhi 110 044
India

SAGE Ltd.
1 Oliver's Yard
55 City Road
London EC1Y 1SP
United Kingdom

SAGE Asia-Pacific Pte. Ltd.
33 Pekin Street #02-01
Far East Square
Singapore 048763

Printed in the United States of America

Library of Congress Cataloging-in-Publication Data

Deal, Terrence E.
Reviving the soul of teaching: balancing metrics and magic / Terrence E. Deal, Peggy Deal Redman.
    p. cm.
Includes bibliographical references and index.
ISBN 978-1-4129-4051-1 (cloth : acid-free paper)
ISBN 978-1-4129-4052-8 (pbk. : acid-free paper)
    1. Teaching.   2. Teachers.   I. Redman, Peggy Deal.   II. Title.

LB1025.3.D415 2009
371.102—dc22   2008004880

This book is printed on acid-free paper.

08   09   10   11   12   10   9   8   7   6   5   4   3   2   1

Acquisitions Editor: Debra Stollenwerk
Editorial Assistants: Jordan Barbakow, Allison Scott
Production Editor: Appingo Publishing Services
Cover Designer: Lisa Miller

Contents

Foreword

For as long as there have been schools in America, there have always been children who have been left behind. As I think back to my school days beginning in the 1950s and extending through the early 1960s, I wonder what happened to all those students who just fell by the way. I remember Randy, a wonderfully talented baseball player who had the misfortune of being born on the wrong side of the tracks. He struggled in school and dropped out before he had the opportunity to display his talents as a member of our high school team. The last time I saw Randy, he was driving a taxicab. I can still picture him slouched way down low in the front seat of his cab while taking a long drag off of an unfiltered cigarette. Randy hadn't shaved in several days, and he had put on a lot of weight. He looked bad—nothing at all like the gifted, young athlete who had vanished many years before I saw him wasting away in the front seat of his taxicab on that bright, sunny spring morning long ago.

Lots of kids like Randy suffered the same fate. I remember a brother and sister, Jack and Mary, who were in my grade in school. They were tough kids from out in the country who left school when they were twelve or thirteen. I heard that Jack became a tree surgeon, but I have no idea what happened to Mary. I can still recall a beautiful young girl, Faye, who left school and married in the ninth grade. Somebody told me she died quite young of cervical cancer, but I don't know that for sure. And there was Neil, one of my best friends up until high school. Neil was bright, but lacked direction in his life. He dropped out of school after the ninth grade, and I have no idea what happened to him after that. Truthfully, I don't recall very many, if any, special needs children who became somebody. Nobody knows because back then they never even got started. The point is that there are now, and have always been, countless children who have failed in school and, at the same time, have been failed by their schools. Since there have been schools in America, these children have all been left behind and are still falling between the cracks. And every single one of them is a tragedy. Haunting images of these wasted lives influenced my decision to become a teacher.

Given that most Americans have had school experiences like mine, where they witnessed so many of their schoolmates shunted to the side, it is little wonder that a federal education initiative billed as No Child Left Behind (NCLB) would capture the imagination of a nation. After all, who among us would want to see even a single child left looking helplessly lost and forlorn standing alone by the side of the road that leads to future happiness and success? With their flowery language, the champions of NCLB have skillfully painted a beautiful picture of an idealized American school system where every child succeeds and goes on to live a happy and productive life. But sometimes legislators seem to forget that the bona fide job of preventing kids from tumbling from the precipice is carried out in local classrooms—not in national or state capitols. It is classroom teachers who stand sentinel and pull children back from the abyss.

On July 1, 2007, I retired from a career as a professional educator that began as an English teacher at a rural junior/senior high school in north central Florida in the late 1960s. I have always felt extremely fortunate and privileged to have spent my professional life in education. If asked why, I always tell people that I have never had a day that I didn't want to go to work. Although when I'm being totally honest, I have to admit that there have been some days I have enjoyed a good deal less than others!

I took a position teaching English to sixth, seventh, eighth, and ninth graders at the school where I had student taught and have never really looked back. The reason I have never looked back is that once I started teaching *for real*, I soon discovered something that has drawn so many to a career in teaching. I discovered that my students really needed me to help them learn what they needed to know to live happy and productive lives. I guess one could say that students taught me that *the most important thing in life is living a life that matters!* Teachers matter because their lives have a profound and lasting impact on the young lives they are privileged to touch each and every day. I couldn't help those left behind in my early memories. But I did make a difference for those I taught during my classroom career.

Now, in my semiretirement I conduct workshops. Often I ask participants to list the eight or ten people who have had the most impact on their development as human beings—a sort of de facto "Personal Board of Directors." Then I ask the members of the group to raise their hands, in turn, if they have a medical doctor on their personal list, an engineer, an attorney, or a business executive. For each of these categories, one or two hands may go up in the room. Then I ask the group how many have a teacher on their list. Without fail, every person in the room raises a hand. Then I ask how many have two or more teachers on their list. Again, all, or almost all the hands in the room go up. In any group, there will always be those with three, four, five, or more teachers on their lists of people who have mattered. This is a powerful illustration that teachers live lives that count because they have such a powerful and lasting influence on the lives of others. It's an irrefutable fact that this influence goes far beyond the teaching of content knowledge.

In *Reviving the Soul of Teaching: Balancing Metrics and Magic*, Terrence E. Deal and Peggy Deal Redman do a brilliant job of deciphering exactly what it is about teaching that gives it such power to change lives. They caution the reader that masterful teaching should not just be recognized—it must be cherished, protected, and preserved. Terry and Peggy remind us that we must not lose sight of the magical essence that is the hallmark of masterful teaching in our quest to raise standards. They argue eloquently for a balanced approach to raising standards that also acknowledges the fragile nature of teaching that borders on the sublime.

In all honesty, I simply can't imagine two people who are better equipped to tell this particular story than are Peggy and Terry. Both have won numerous awards for their masterful, magical teaching over long and distinguished careers in K–12 public schools and higher education institutions as well. I've personally been mesmerized watching Terry Deal work with students in various settings and have often said of Peggy that "[i]f I could pick one person in the entire world to teach me how to teach, that person would be Peggy Deal Redman!"

Reviving the Soul of Teaching: Balancing Metrics and Magic is one of the most readable books I have read in a very long time. These two writers are accomplished "tribal storytellers" and do they have a story to tell! The language is beautiful and compelling, but at the same time, the words ring true. You will find yourself nodding your head in agreement as Deal and Redman peel away the layers of NCLB to reveal the veiled underbelly of the legislation that could effectively erode the very essence of teaching—unless we are careful to balance the drive for standards with respect and appreciation for the art and magic of teaching in its purest form. You will laugh at the description of Walter F. Myers performing the magical rituals that are at the heart of masterful teaching. You will sigh when you read the words of master teachers who have become frustrated and disillusioned by being forced to teach in a manner that deprives children of the best that these teachers have to offer them. And you will feel sorry for the children who are missing the most important lessons that could ever be learned in school while they are being mindlessly drilled and tested. But most of all, you will feel inspired by Deal and Redman's clarion call for teachers to take a more active leadership role in helping to shape the future of the profession to ensure that the magical essence of teaching is preserved for and revered by future generations.

This is an important book for anyone who genuinely cares about children and what happens to them in schools. The central message is that good teaching is much more than a science. When teaching is performed at its highest level, it is mystery, magic, and majesty all rolled into one. The authors' words will inspire any teacher who desires to "teach the way my heart and soul tells me is right."

This book makes it clear that while standards are important, we must be careful to seek balance lest we destroy the essential fabric of an educational system—magical teaching— that has made America the great nation that it is today. Peggy and Terry remind us that "to a good teacher, a child is more than a test score" and offer the admonition that "schools don't need more reform, they need a good dose of revival to reconnect with mystical beliefs about the ennobling of purpose, greater cause, and higher calling within this profession." Deal and Redman end with an eloquent entreaty to all of us who are called to teach to demand the respect we deserve as teachers in order to "restore the magic and soul of teaching and learning that is our primary challenge." After reading this book, I realize more than ever what a lofty privilege it is to be *"just a teacher!"*

Leonard O. Pellicer
Distinguished Professor Emeritus

Preface

A Family of Teachers

The two of us come from an extended family of teachers. It didn't start out that way, as our forbearers were originally farmers working a meager homesteaded quarter in Rock Lake, North Dakota. In fact, the Deal "quarter" can be recalled today by residents of the small town close to the Canadian border still without a paved main street. Our grandmother's vision was that her children would leave the farm for a college education and a better life. She embodied the values of schooling. She wasn't opposed to tilling the soil, but she saw a greater good in cultivating the human spirit. As she pushed her brood off the farm, one by one, they gravitated toward careers in teaching. Of the seven siblings in our father's family, all seven became teachers. Most of our relatives are teachers. Both of our fathers were teachers, one of our mothers was a teacher.

Ironically, growing up in this family dominated by teachers, no one talked much about teaching. It was embedded deeply in the yeasty atmosphere of the family unit. Our love for the profession just somehow seeped into our pores. When it came time to declare a college major, most of our generation picked teaching. As we entered the profession the reality proved to be different from the experience of our parents' era, but there were also common threads that spanned the generations. We learned that a classroom is a classroom wherever it happens to be located. We also learned some very basic principles about good teaching. Chief among these were that caring, compassion, and inspiration play a critical role in genuine teaching and learning; that teachers are important for who they are as well as for what they teach; and that students bring their own unique gifts to the relationship.

Our generation taught in many different types of schools. Some were affluent; others were tough inner-city assignments. Some taught in primary grades; others taught in secondary settings. Like our parents, we didn't talk much about teaching at family gatherings, but something clearly trickled down because many in our children's generation are teachers. Their conception of teaching closely mirrors that of the two generations that preceded them. And so the tradition is carried forward.

The problem is that our children's generation has to fight for values commonly accepted in earlier eras. Long-term missions such as caring, compassion, encouragement, and building character now too often take second place to short-term goals of standardized performance and high-stakes testing. More and more, teachers are pushed to become dispensers of a limited range of only partially relevant facts. They have little time to share themselves and are seen as technically interchangeable. The active role played in the past by students has been supplanted by an emphasis on them as passive receptors of knowledge. Whatever they have to offer is largely irrelevant to the mandated lock-step curriculum prevalent in many schools today. Our family's unwritten credo was to draw out students' potential, not drum in facts and figures.

This fundamental shift in schooling has been underway for several decades. Reforming schools is the key battle cry of today's politicians. Even though many would agree that, in the past, they have screwed up, they won't give up. The beat goes on and on and on. The most recent and troublesome manifestation of this cycle of standardization and measurement is No Child Left Behind. At its core it assumes that test scores are the only measure for judging a school's performance, and it punishes those who don't measure up.

Three generations of Deals are among the critics of what this legislation is doing to teaching and learning. It is undermining the essence of imagination and creativity that are at the core of our strength as a nation. Very few are standing up to champion the emotional and spiritual side of schooling. Someone needs to call attention to the delight and faith that captures the hearts and souls of students and teachers. That's why we wrote this book. We know that our grandmother would be proud and that generations of Deals are standing shoulder to shoulder with us as we undertake this quest. We have been taught to teach this way, and we are going to make sure that we do not lose the traditional values that make teaching one of the most sacred professions. Our argument is based primarily on our personal experience as teachers, a lot of hours logged in schools and classrooms, and our direct contact with other educators across America. Where possible, we will draw on the work of others but make no claim to present a rigorous body of knowledge to back us up. This book is personal and at times we will become polemical. It is because we believe so ardently in the need to balance the mechanical and mystical aspects of teaching.

This is a battle we are fully prepared to engage and are determined to win. Our objective is not to overthrow accountability, but rather to counterweight its overemphasis with a fresh breath of passion and zest. Too often, policymakers and educators look to the business world for direction when top-performing businesses themselves seek parity between metrics and magic. Max DePree (1989), founder of Herman Miller and a well-known business writer, captures the issue elegantly, "Being faithful is more important than being successful. Corporations can and should have a redemptive purpose. We need to weigh the pragmatic in the clarifying light of the moral. We must understand that reaching our potential is more important than reaching our goal" (p. 69).

DePree is not a lone wolf in the business community. Other leaders of successful enterprises pepper their language with too-oft forgotten terms such as *soul, spirit, heart, faith, hope,* and *love.* Higher calling, ennobling purpose, and greater cause stir people's passion to strive to fulfill a shared hallowed potential.

It seems sad that this spiritual-like idiom is alive in organizations that fly aircrafts, brew coffee, make pet food, manufacture cars or adhesives, and formulate remedies, but absent in how we talk about our children and schools. Dominance of standards, bottom-line results, measurable outcomes, and pay for performance seem foreign in an institution devoted to the nurturing and shaping of the next generation. Teaching is more an art form than a mechanical assembly line. We hope you will join us in bringing more balance and buoyancy to one of our society's most righteous, majestic undertakings.

The book's thesis plays out in a series of chapters, each devoted to one of the challenges we need to confront in rescuing education from its trendy, perilous journey. The Introduction, "Teaching: Past and Prologue," traces where we've been, where we are, and highlights a fork in the road ahead. Chapter 1, "Reviving the Soul of Teaching," compares two conceptions of teaching, emphasizing literature that focuses on the heart and soul of the profession. Chapter 2, "Making a Difference: The Core of Teaching," examines what it means to make a difference through several examples. Chapter 3, "School Reform: A Ground Level Perspective," contrasts the views of once removed policymakers with teachers, students, and parents who experience changes directly. Chapter 4, "Being Real: The Authentic Teacher," shows how who a teacher is carries as much influence as what they teach. Chapter 5, "You Gotta Believe," highlights the importance of teachers believing in themselves and having faith and confidence in what they do. Chapter 6, "Setting the Spirit Free," shifts attention from the individual teacher and classroom to the school as a potentially spirit-filled context that fires the collective imagination and touches the heart and soul of the community. Chapter 7, "Speaking Up: Voices from the Trenches," encourages teachers to capture the ears of policymakers by aggressively mounting a chorus rather than whining or leaving the profession. Chapter 8, "Charting a New Course," provides a glimmer of a new direction in moving from the endless drift of school reform in search of some promising new destinations.

We conclude without any new policies to pronounce or innovative specific steps to take. As the Wizard of Oz once said to the Cowardly Lion, "All you need is confidence in yourself. There is no living thing that is not afraid when it faces danger. True courage is facing danger when you are afraid, and that kind of courage you have in plenty" (Baum, p. 114). The ball is now in the court of America's teachers and administrators. Give it your best shot. Our grandmother would be behind you all the way. So are we.

Acknowledgments

This book is precious to us as more than a synthesis of ideas we hope others will enjoy and apply. It represents the heritage of a family devoted to teaching. The joy of teaching was passed on to us as others inherit money or property. Now it becomes our ancestral obligation to share our bequest with others. Several people have helped us as we ambled toward the finish line.

Debra Stollenwerk has been more than an acquisitions editor. She has shaped the direction of this book and provided several types of helpful support as we moved along. Wendy Wood masterfully transformed our drafts into the obligatory format.

It is impossible to write anything without the thoughts of long time intellectual partner, Lee Bolman, seeping into the prose. Tom McGuire's low-key, sensible, and professional grounding helped keep us on track. Leonard Pellicer, in addition to writing the foreword, served as a caring sounding board as we developed our ideas.

We appreciate the inspiration of the group of authors whose tenacity and courage keeps the true meaning of teaching alive at an ominous time of competing methods. We also thank all of the great teachers we have encountered in our experience—as students, colleagues, and icons.

In our nuclear families, several people deserve special credit. Our brother and cousin, Larry Deal, exemplifies the best of this book. Jerry Redman, Larry Redman, and Donna Redman Nasmyth keep us attuned to the important things in life. Jane Deal Rice, as a chef, treats food as students. Sandra Deal's love and intellect have been inspirational as the book evolved.

About the Authors

Terrence E. Deal began his career as a teacher in Pomona, California. He received his BA from La Verne College, his MA from California State College at Los Angeles, and his PhD from Stanford University. After a five-year stint as an English and Social Studies teacher at Pomona's Fremont Junior High School, he went on to teach in northern California at Pacific Grove High School. His teaching career continued at the university level: Stanford University, Harvard University, and Vanderbilt University, and the University of Southern California as an Irving R. Melbo Professor. Among his most prized awards are a number of Crystal Apple teaching awards from Peabody College, and the Sarratt Award for excellence in undergraduate teaching at Vanderbilt University. He has written over thirty books, the latest of which is *The Wizard and the Warrior*, coauthored with Lee Bolman. He is currently retired and an amateur winemaker in San Luis Obispo, California's Edna Valley.

Peggy Deal Redman began her teaching career as a junior high teacher in Pomona at Marshall Junior High School. She received her BA from La Verne College and her MEd and EdD from the University of La Verne. Her career includes seventeen years as a teacher of elementary school gifted and primary school students in the Bonita Unified School District. She was honored by the Alumni Association with the Distinguished Professor Award and has been recognized by her colleagues with the Excellence in Teaching Award. Her book, *Don't Smile Until December and Other Myths About Classroom Teaching,* was nominated for recognition by *Foreword* magazine. She is currently Director of Teacher Education at the University of La Verne, where she has been for twenty-five years. She holds the La Fetra Family Endowed Chair in Excellence in Teaching.

Introduction
Teaching: Past and Prologue

In 1932 William Waller, a sociologist, wrote a book about teaching. Anyone who picked it up now and ignored the ancient cover would swear he was writing about schools today:

> *Schools have a culture that is definitely their own. There are, in the school, complex rituals of personal relationships, a set of folkways, mores, and irrational sanctions, a moral code based upon them. There are games, which are sublimated, wars, teams, and an elaborate set of ceremonies concerning them. There are traditions, and traditionalists waging their world-old battle against innovators. (p. 96)*

At the beginning of the 2007 school year, Garrison Keillor, of the radio program *A Prairie Home Companion,* aired a special back-to-school broadcast. He began by reminiscing about blackboards, white chalk, familiar smells, and favorite teachers. A song titled "We Shall Never Forget" set the tone of the broadcast. He ended with the story of the funeral of Miss Lewis, a feared yet favorite English teacher. A listener without a tear in his or her eye would have been in the minority. He hit a chord at the heart of teaching. In one way or another, none of us will ever forget our school days. But in our fast-paced, complex world, many of us do lose contact with the debt we owe to those who shaped our lives. In one of America's finest school systems, they didn't forget.

Fairfax County, Virginia, is one of America's premier school systems. In 1985, the administrative team produced a video chronicling the district's history from its inception in 1922 to the present. The production opens with Louise Harrison, a teacher in one of Fairfax's original one-room schoolhouses. She describes her early experience in the following:

> *I was fresh out of high school. I graduated in June of 1923 and in September of that year, I started teaching. That was in the little one-room school at Navy. Of course, there was no electricity or anything like that. We also had no water and no well on the property. In fact, the children had to carry water from several houses down the road. I was responsible for having the fire made, for cleaning up the building, and doing all sorts of things like that. I even very often got down on my hands and knees washed the floor and oiled it. They did furnish us a broom. As far as I remember we had no mop or anything like that, just a plain broom. But if you could see the mud on the children's feet, you'd know a mop wouldn't do much good and the floor was pretty rough too . . . There were seven grades I had beginning with the primer through the seventh grade. I had only one boy in the seventh grade, however. You know it's sorta like teaching today. You group your children according to their ability to do, as well as where they stood on their work. You couldn't get around them unless you did group them.*

Using Louise Harrison as a historical marker, teaching has come a long way from its early ancestry. Yet embedded in her story are some recognizable themes now dressed in modern raiment. The center of learning is still the classroom, housing one teacher and a group of students. Overall, there is less variability in students' ages in individual classrooms but much more spread in ethnic and cultural origins. There are some structural differences. The stand-alone, one-room classroom is now formally embedded in a school with several classrooms. The faculty is overseen officially by a principal, assisted by a support staff, and some of Louise's maintenance duties are now the job of the school custodian. Yet in modern classrooms, something present in the one-room schoolhouse too often is missing. It's not tangible nor easily expressed and goes well beyond the old belief that teachers had eyes in the back of their heads and other tales. It falls outside the rational and is centered more in the magical or spiritual realm.

HISTORICAL ROOTS

What's too often missing today is a bedrock belief and unshakable faith among teachers, parents, the local community, and the nation at large that teachers can make a significant difference in the character as well as the cognition of a young person. Its absence creates a contemporary void that was once filled. Shared faith, based on religion and capitalism, was dominant in Horace Mann's common school movement. It kindled a zealous, widespread commitment to assure a universal education for every child. The movement also imbued education and educators with a distinctive moral authority: "Leadership in education was often seen as a calling similar to that of church missionary" (Tyack & Hansot, 1982, p. 16). "The teacher is the prophet of the true God and the sharer in the true kingdom of God" (p. 3).

The common school provided the basic 3Rs, but added religion to shape a student's values and moral fiber. There was more going on in Louise Harrison's one-room domain than an emphasis on developing fundamental skills. From her obvious dedication, it is not much of a stretch to conclude that she was in the business of shaping young lives.

Faith and belief in public education continued as the religious zealotry of the common school movement melded into schools built on the tenets of science and modern business practices. Ellwood Cubberly (1916) and others launched their effort to put teaching on a more rational, efficient, scientific, and business-like foundation. Schools were clustered into districts governed by local school boards, working through a superintendent to reassure that policies found their way into practice. The local school became a bureaucratic unit supervised officially by a principal. Teachers were cast as workers. Their instructional toil was supposedly based on science and played to an audience that believed in both empirical knowledge and business acumen. Public confidence in schools remained intact. But both business and science also had a built-in method for undermining confidence based on faith and belief—measuring results. As the tandem of business and science-based methods failed to produce the promised yields, people's conviction began to wane. This produced a growing discord of dissatisfaction, especially among parents and the wider citizenry. Critics clamored for improvement.

The social experimentation of the late 1960s and early 1970s produced pockets of unconventional schools with a small inner sanctum of supporters and true believers. But these noble and inspired blips burst on the scene as lions and exited as neutered house pets, absent tangible evidence of their efficacy. To be sure, the student-centered, learning-by-doing philosophy of unconventional schools yielded some dramatic transformations of students previously written off. But this anecdotal confirmation did not wash among those who were not zealots and wanted more rigorous proof. Schools without walls, alternative schools, and progressive methods all had their place in the sun (Deal & Nolan, 1978), but each ran afoul of the dominant image of the school as a place of production and source of an educated labor pool. Most of these righteous experiments either failed outright or became a battleground of special interests vying to impose their parochial values onto public education. A coalition of business people loomed as the most vocal and forceful.

CURRENT REALITIES

History is important to understanding where we have been, assessing where we are, and forecasting the direction we need to follow:

All people and institutions are the product of history (defined as past events). And whether they are aware of it or not, all people use history (defined as an interpretation of past events) when they make choices about the present and future. (Tyack & Hansot, 1982, p. 6)

In recent memory, political rhetoric assigns education high priority. In presidential campaigns education is touted as a top issue. The last three U.S. presidents have given educational reform priority on the national agenda. No one could become the governor of a state today without proclaiming education as a matter of the greatest magnitude. But beyond the rhetoric is a cacophony of values staking claim on where to go next. One approach decisively has taken the high ground. Schools are now required to adopt programs based on national standards and to show results on uniform standardized tests. This national legislation has a worthy objective that is hard to dispute: Every child in America should be given a chance to succeed. No Child Left Behind (NCLB) is the most recent in a seemingly never-ending policy parade to bring public schools up to snuff with technical, scientific logic and hardheaded business practices.

The major investment of scarce resources in NCLB reflects a widespread conviction that schools are the logical place to solve all of our social ills. As John Dewey pointed out in 1916, "The public school system is the willing pack horse of our social system. It is the true hero of the refrain 'let George do it'" (as cited in Cuban, 2004, p. 164).

The problem is that the packhorse is often not that willing or heroic. As a result, policymakers' good intentions invariably fall short of expectations or produce consequences neither foreseen nor intended. Since the dawning of the campaign to put schools on a more business-scientific footing, the tempo of initiatives to attain that objective has increased. Volumes of research spell out data-driven instructional techniques for improving test scores. Emphasis is placed on the direct, concrete, and short-term consequences of teaching. Almost every new reform strategy relies heavily on business acumen and scientific rigor to plot the pathway to improvement. Very often, new efforts are merely old castoffs given a new name and updated with cosmetic touchups.

As just one historical example, the 1970s produced a then high-touted movement to have teachers specify their pedagogical objectives in computable terms. This effort was given the acronym PPBS (Planning, Programming, and Budgeting System). Although it was somewhat discredited in the business world even then, teachers were nonetheless set to work writing succinct, measurable objectives for their instructional goals. Harry Wolcott's (1971) meticulous description of one district's experiment with PPBS told a familiar story of what was happening elsewhere. The effort was a bust; teachers struggled to write precise aims for efforts that were unrelated to their traditional classroom practices. Time was wasted, tempers flared, and the project quietly went the way of most educational reforms. Wolcott concluded his in-depth analysis of the disaster with a chilling epitaph: "How can we keep this from happening again?" Since 1970, it has happened again and again. Schools are asked to shove teachers in a more businesstechnical direction and to document their accomplishments.

Yogi Berra, in his commonsense wisdom once remarked, "We're hopelessly lost, but we're sure making good time." That pretty much sums up where we are in education today. We have lost our way, but we keep ratcheting up wellintended efforts to improve teaching and learning. But as an inadvertent consequence, the American public's faith in education is ebbing and, even more disturbing, many teachers no longer believe in themselves. Would Louise Harrison, of Fairfax County, have described her role as many teachers do today: "I'm just a teacher"?

SCHOOLS AS ORGANIZATIONS

Whenever things go awry, we invariably want to pin the blame somewhere or on someone. Policymakers fault "laggard" educators who don't care about student achievement—especially among minorities. The teachers, in turn, assign culpability to "out-of- touch," politically motivated legislators, poorly motivated students, or disinterested parents. Parents watching the ongoing culpability ping-pong contest either join one side or the other—or just want whoever is guilty punished—and then get on with it. Ironically, individuals are not the root of the problem—rather, it is a widespread misconception of schools as organizations. The dominant mind-set characterizes schools as production-oriented learning factories. Raw materials (students) pass through a predetermined methodical process (teaching) and emerge as finished products (literate, skilled workers). The emphasis is on systemizing the technical core, streamlining the production line, and routinizing the role of workers (teachers). The enterprise is judged almost entirely on measurable results. The language of this image speaks volumes about its governing assumptions.

The less prevalent view characterizes schools as institutions where myth and faith trump logic and facts. From this perspective, it's hard to imagine a church or synagogue held accountable for salvation rates. It becomes much easier to understand why hospitals don't publish their morbidity-mortality statistics. When goals and results are multiple, hard to measure, or the ties between cause and effect are unclear or remote, judging how well an enterprise is doing is largely a matter of belief and faith. Test scores calculate only a small slice of what schools are all about. The rest is determined by how well a school fits the mythical image of a "good" or "up-to-date" operation.

If a school "looks right" people assume it must be working; if it deviates too far from "goodness," they demand some proof. Schools respond to reform mandates by symbolically demonstrating conformance. On the surface they showcase innovations of the moment to appease multiple interest groups. Behind the façade, teachers and principals find refuge in an archetypical symbolic or cultural cocoon that imbues their efforts with merit and stability. As the outside pressures roil, classrooms housing the age-old organic relationship between teachers and students stay the course relatively undisturbed.

Their immunity had prevailed until national policy fell in love with the factory logic and, with the blessing of key constituencies, put some teeth into legislation and strong armed schools to comply. This started to erode the logic of faith and belief and put education into an unusual downward tailspin, at least temporarily. With the introduction of technology in classrooms, for example, some teachers are beginning to wonder if they will be replaced by computers, interactive programs, and an aide who keeps students under control. In *Goodbye, Mr. and Ms. Chips*, Nancy Ginsburg Gill (2007) laments,

> *While they may in fact raise test scores somewhat, scripted lessons can be deadly to children eager to learn more than what is covered on the test for their grade level. These schools can be even more mind-numbing for teachers who have been attracted to the profession by a desire to engender in their students a passion for learning. (p. 35)*

BALANCING MEASUREMENT AND MAGIC

The key problem today in education is restoring a sense of equilibrium or balance to an eternal paradox. All organizations are like teeter-totters seeking a workable point of symmetry between standards and spirit, profits and passion, measurement and magic. When the seesaw tips too far in either direction, problems mushroom. Schools may now be reaching the "tipping" point when a disease becomes an epidemic (Gladwell, 2002); in other words, when the factory logic of systems and results overwhelms the magic and mystery of teaching and learning.

Contrary to popular opinion, schools are not the only organizations that seem to have reached the brink. Ongoing efforts to restore equilibrium between technical and symbolic weights are spread across sectors. The struggle to maintain symmetry between standards and soul is currently making headlines in business, an exemplar of virtue often invoked for schools to emulate. Too often the wrong businesses are held up as models to imitate. Executives are prone to recommend for schools guidelines they don't always heed themselves.

As an example, Lou Gerstner, Jr., former CEO of IBM is a leader in the educational accountability drive. Yet in his role at IBM's turnaround, he came to appreciate the important role of history and symbols in business success. In his first days at the company, he seemed the hardheaded businessman people expected. At one of his first press conferences he reinforced his image by commenting clearly, "The last thing that IBM needs is a vision." At some point during his time as CEO he "fell in love with IBM" (Gerstner, 2002, p. 279). As he revisited the company's history, he discovered that Thomas Watson, Sr., its founder, had coined a set of values that still made sense. But, as time passed, the company had drifted from its early roots to become a rigid, self-sealing feudal bureaucracy. His challenge shifted from imposing something new to reviving and restoring sheen to what had once made IBM a walkaway success.

STARBUCKS AND 3M: RESTORING BALANCE

Two comparable business examples seem especially applicable to today's efforts to put schools back on track: Starbucks and 3M. The Starbucks Corporation has become the world's primary purveyor of coffee. Don't like the outlet close to you? Walk three blocks to another one. Besides its distinctive blend of coffee beans, Starbucks is famous for its unique experience and special touch. Chairman and founder Howard Schultz (1997) has not been shy about trumpeting the company's unique character:

If people relate to the company they work for, if they form an emotional tie to it and buy into its dreams, they will pour their hearts into making it better. When employees have self-esteem and self-respect they can contribute so much more to their company, to their family, to the world . . . . The key is heart. I pour my heart into every cup of coffee and so do my partners at Starbucks. When customers sense that, they respond in kind. (Pour Your Heart Into It, *pp. 6–8)*

In 2007 Schultz's tone took a sharp turn. Growth and automation had shifted the balance between romance and rationality. The important intangibles that defined Starbuck's spirit were endangered. Schultz fired off a memo to key executives. Sites, he lamented, "no longer have the soul of the past and reflect a chain of stores vs. the warm feeling of a neighborhood store" (Gross, 2007, p. M1). Automatic espresso machines replaced the authentic, artful *barista* hand-operated models. Putting coffee in flavor-locked packages kept the product fresher, but caused the stores to lose the distinctive aroma of coffee beans. Concerns for efficiency had tipped the balance of genuineness in an unacceptable direction. Schultz's memo was aimed at restoring parity: "It's time to get back to the core and make the changes that are necessary to evoke the heritage, the tradition, and the passion that we all have for the Starbuck's experience" (Allison, 2004).

3M supplies a comparable case under different circumstances. Based in St. Paul, Minnesota, the company has been widely renowned for its creativity. Its soul, its bedrock identity, has been historically anchored to the generation of new ideas. It all began with the dogged persistence of an enterprising employee pursuing a personal pet project, a transparent tape that would affix firmly to nearly any surface. He was ordered to work on his assigned project but ignored his superiors and continued unrelentingly to track his dream. The outcome was Scotch Tape, a product that returned enormous profits for the company and serves an ongoing example for other employees to tag along.

An innovative company tolerates mistakes, a natural by-product of creativity. Errors somewhere in the process once produced a batch of adhesive that failed to fully adhere. An employee serendipitously discovered that paper coated with the botched product worked perfectly to mark his place in church hymnals and other books where he wanted to keep his place temporarily without leaving unwanted residue. That, of course, was the origin of Post-it Notes, another of the company's wildly successful products.

Like Starbuck's, in the late 1990s, 3M began to drift from its core. Productivity dipped and efficiency began to sag noticeably. For the first time 3M's board went outside to select a new CEO. James McNerney, one of Jack Welch's protégés at GE, was chosen to get the company back on course. McNerney wasted little time in importing from GE Six Sigma, a systematic process like Total Quality Management (TQM), using rigorous statistical analysis to pinpoint production defects and increase efficiency. The essence of Six Sigma is define, measure, analyze, improve, and control. While the process has enjoyed considerable success in improving production of tangible goods, it fails when the process and outcomes, like creativity or innovation, are ambiguous and hard to quantify and assess (Hindo, 2007).

Initially, the process seemed to pay off in production, earnings, and stock price. McNerney used the process to slash expenditures and reduce the size of the workforce. But then innovation and creativity, once hallmarks of the 3M culture, began to erode. McNerney folded his tent and moved to Boeing, leaving 3M in shambles. An employee commented, "What is remarkable is how fast a culture can be torn apart. McNerney didn't kill it because he wasn't here long enough. But if he had been much longer, I think he would have" (Hindo, 2007, p. 10). Another employee concluded, "When you value sameness more than you value creativity, I think you undermine the heart and soul of a company like 3M" (p. 10). Both Starbucks and 3M suffered because of the imbalance between rationality and intangibility. Starbuck's disparity was a result of growth and automation, 3M's because of the negative side effects of an overly rigid process to standardize and measure outcomes. If contemporary corporations are often out of whack, what about schools? All three business examples highlight lessons with direct application to education.

The main problem with today's schools is the conspicuous imbalance between rationality and spirituality, production and passion. Reform efforts have woefully overweighted one end of the seesaw at the expense of the other. Standards and test results are overwhelming other important roles teachers play in the lives of young people. The most important value at risk in the incessant messing around with public schools is the intangible, often indirect influence that a teacher may have on the course of a child's life. It's not usually quantifiable. It sometimes goes unrecognized until an adult realizes the powerful difference a teacher made. It sometimes is never realized. Frank McCourt (2005) poignantly spells out what too often happens to teachers:

> I had an English teacher, Miss Smith, who really inspired me. She used to say that if she reached one child in her forty years of teaching it would make it all worthwhile. She'd die happy. The inspiring English teacher then fades into the gray shadows to eke out her days on a penny-pinching pension, dreaming of the one child she may have reached. Dream on teacher. You will not be celebrated. (pp. 4–5)

Ironically, as the teacher dreams, a student somewhere cherishes the memory of a teacher whose inspiration lingers on. He would love to tell her how much she had meant to him, but he doesn't know how. This tragedy, an unwelcome by-product of years of misdirected school reform, should never be allowed to stand. Somehow we need to put things back on a more even keel, to once again have public schools in which faith flourishes and to reinvigorate teachers who ardently believe in themselves and the lofty value of their work.

1

Reconfirming the Soul of Teaching

Imagine yourself as a veteran teacher with thirty years of classroom experience. You've seen more than your share of innovations that glitter then fizzle. Years ago you experienced the thrill of becoming involved with a new district project, but it didn't pan out and you got burned. The scars still linger and you're reluctant to risk getting disappointed or hurt again. Better to shut your classroom door and deal with kids in ways your experience has taught will work. After all, why did you become a teacher in the first place? Not to get caught up in every new fad that comes along. Now you don't seem to have a choice. You're feeling pressured by your principal to "teach to the tests." That violates your code of what's right. But so much of what you read and hear says you're wrong. Still, you forge ahead. You pride yourself in viewing each of your young charges as a promise. You do whatever you can to nudge every individual in the right direction. Your motto is "To teach is to touch a life forever." You still believe that, but it doesn't seem to stack up against the realities of hard numerical evidence: percentages, stanines, and quartiles. Like many other colleagues, you'll just bide your time. This too shall pass. If not, retirement is always an option. Then what?

The reality is that there are a lot of teachers today who feel this way. To a good teacher, a child is more than a number. The same danger, focusing only on what can be summarized in statistical form, haunts other professions today. A lawyer's client is more than a billing hour. A physician's patient has a life beyond a diagnosis or a disease to be cured. Teaching, like law and medicine, began as a calling, a noble profession with a higher purpose. Reviving that spirit to achieve parity with factory-like images is the less traveled path we now need to follow.

Where does a teacher turn for support and nourishment? Wherever you look, the heart and soul of teaching seems to run a distant second place to the nuts and bolts. Artistry succumbs to the lure of scientific and technical certainty. The formal knowledge base of teaching today seems devoted almost exclusively to methods of instruction, classroom management, or evaluation. Rigorous research-based knowledge is touted as better than grounded experience-derived wisdom. Most research and commentary attempt to link teaching with quantifiable outcomes—teacher as technician or classroom manager.

But there is a parallel conception of teaching conveyed by a multitude of books and articles. Prospective teachers rarely see this yeasty aspect in their preparation programs. Too many seasoned pros are so ground down and shellshocked by relentless reform that this smoldering, idealistic notion is a faded memory. So much of what is available to read as a pick-me-up is dominated by lifeless, technical jargon. But the idea of the teacher as valued mentor lives on, kept alive by tenacious authors who won't cave in.

SOULFUL WISDOM

The artful, teacher-friendly literature emphasizes the expressive, emotional, spiritual side of the profession. Roland Barth (2001) compares the two:

One set [of writings] consists of the things these teachers must do that give the illusion of compliance and will ensure they do not get fired: fifteen minutes a week of drug instruction, drilling students in preparation for the standardized tests, and so on.

The second set of books consists of those matters educators passionately believe in. This is why they entered the profession. These are the things they do that enable them to maintain their self-respect, integrity, passion, and heart: relating a recent summer spent in Italy to a unit on the Renaissance, assisting a student who wants to devise an unusual science experiment. Unfortunately, these days few teachers experience much congruence [or sense of balance] between the two sets of books. (pp. 4–5)

A journey through the second set of books or articles brings us closer to the existential underbelly of the teaching profession. Rather than flat and pale gray, the language is poetic and hot pink. Words such as heart, soul, passion, and love pepper the pages. Vigor replaces rigor, zest is substituted for sternness, inspiration is valued over discipline, art supercedes science, and play dominates toil in this image of teaching and teachers. A premium is placed on long-term influence rather that short-term effects. Teachers' moral virtue overshadows their official authority.

Parker Palmer (1998) writes,

The connections made by good teachers are held not in their methods but in their hearts—meaning heart in its ancient sense, as the place where intellect and emotion and spirit and will converge in the human self . . . teaching tugs at the heart, opens the heart, even breaks the heart—and the more one loves teaching, the more heartbreaking it can be. The courage to teach is the courage to keep one's heart open in those very moments when the heart is asked to hold more than it is able so that teacher and students and subject can be woven into the fabric of community that learning, and leaving, requires. (p. 11)

Roland Barth (2001) concurs:

When I was an elementary school teacher and a principal, my colleagues and I experienced our work as a profession, even a calling. At the turn of the twenty-first century, I'm afraid that for all too many it has become a job. As a calling or profession, education offers much. As a job it offers little . . . . What is needed is an invitation to practitioners to bring a spirit or creativity and invention into the schoolhouse. What is needed is a sense of heart. (p. 5)

Tracy Kidder (1989) concludes, after an in-depth, yearlong study of Chris Zajac, a typical teacher in a traditional New England classroom:

Teachers usually have no way of knowing that they have made a difference in a child's life, even when they have made a dramatic one. But for children who are used to thinking of themselves as stupid or not worth talking to or deserving rape and beatings, a good teacher can provide an astonishing revelation. A good teacher can give a child at least a chance to feel, "She thinks I'm worth something. Maybe I am." Good teachers put snags in the river of children passing by, and over the years, they redirect hundreds of lives. Many people find it easy to imagine unseen webs of malevolent conspiracy in the world, and they are not always wrong. But there is also an innocence that conspires to hold humanity together, and it is made of people who can never fully know the good that they have done. (pp. 212–213)

William Ayers (2001) adds a supportive note:

A teacher needs a brain to break through the cotton wool smothering the mind, to see beyond the blizzard of labels to this specific child, trembling and whole and real, and to this one and then to this. A teacher needs a heart to fully grasp the importance of that gesture, to recognize in the deepest core of your being that every child is precious, each induplicable, the one and only that ever trod this earth, deserving of the best a teacher can give—respect, awe, reverence, commitment. (p. 135)

Writers like Barth (2001), Palmer (1998), Kidder (1989), and Ayers (2001) are adept at capturing the symbolic depths of teaching practice that more technically oriented authors skim over or miss entirely. Rather than providing concrete prescriptions, they emphasize personal soul-searching that consults the heart instead of the head. It has been said that the heart has a mind of its own. It reinforces the craft knowledge that teachers cull from the trial-and-error experience they accumulate over time. Wisdom looks beyond the information teachers impart and focuses on the between-the-lines influence they have on their young charges. This permanent stamp, for better or worse, is the real "take-away" from the hours, months, and years students spend in the classroom. As a vice president of a large corporation commented, "You'll never really remember what teachers taught, the subject matter. But you'll never forget who they were and how they made you feel."

SUPPORTIVE FOLKLORE AND NARRATIVES

The written word, even sensitively and passionately penned, conveys only a portion of what teaching is all about. That's why teachers frequently rely on a venerable oral tradition, passed from generation to generation. Literature is buttressed by stories that reaffirm the elegance and nobility of teaching. Stories are told and retold on the fly and in formal and informal occasions that invite storytellers to spin their tales of triumphs or travails. Either success or failure is fair game since teachers learn from both. More than the written word, stories stick. Listening to these narratives warms the heart and echoes in the soul. But they are like 3M's Scotch Tape rather than Post-it Notes.

In *Made to Stick,* Chip and Dan Heath (2007) highlight the reasons why some ideas endure while others never catch on. Their conclusion is illustrated by contrasting two very different modes of communication. The first emphasizes abstract, matter-of-fact reasoning. Close your book and try to relate to the statement,

Teachers are important because what they convey may have long-lasting consequences for students that may never become obvious until a substantial amount of time has passed and some significant event occurs that calls attention to their important contribution.

Now try a concrete, detailed example with picture words:

I left the classroom anticipating a retirement of sleeping late, tending my roses, and traveling the U.S. and abroad. For awhile it was great and then, with time on my hands, I began to reflect on what my life has meant. What did I have to show for a lot of hours spent with kids? Nothing came up except I had much less retirement income than my neighbors. Then one day the doorbell rang. I opened the door and instantly recognized one of my former students. He had his wife and daughter with him. His wife had made a cake; his daughter presented me with a handmade, primary crayon illustrated certificate, "Thanks for helping my daddy."

Now close your book and ponder how long you'll remember the message.

It is the same exact idea with two very different ways of expressing it. One has little lasting impact; the other has a robust, lingering afterlife. In their book *Crow and Weasel,* Lopez and Pohrt (1998) write,

Remember only this one thing,
The stories people tell have a way of taking care of them.
If stories come to you, care for them.
And learn to give them away when needed.
Sometimes a person needs a story more than food to stay alive.
That is why we put stories in each other's memories.
This is how people care for themselves.

Stories capture those lovely little intangibles that give teaching unique buoyancy and zest. True or not, narratives stick with us. Folklore, told, retold, and embellished over time, transmits the enduring spiritual give and take, connecting the inner lives of those who spend their careers in classrooms. The magical exchange happens in elementary and secondary classrooms, in higher education, and in informal settings outside school. The magic can be traced back to the encounters between guru and novice, craftsman and apprentice, wizard and seeker:

> *Mentors and apprentices are partners in an ancient human dance, and one of teaching's great rewards is to get back on the dance floor. It is the dance of the spiraling generations, in which the old empower the young with their experience and the young empower the old with new life, reweaving the fabric of the human community as they touch and turn. (Palmer, 1998, p. 25)*

Knowledge and tradition are passed on through teaching and learning prances and twirls. But even more important, in the rhythmic frolic the soul of the teacher touches the soul of the student. This intangible intermingling of passion with fond recollections, the occasional chuckle or tear, and a glimmer of direction is tattooed permanently onto the student's heart to be called on when happenstance presents a need. "Today is the day our passion and our dream become one. Because now without a doubt we know that we have the responsibility to grab a young kid by the hand and teach him or her how to find their rightful place in the world" (Gruwell, 1999, p. 262).

BUMBLING PASSION

The two of us know this ancient dance and its enduring traces firsthand. In our freshman year at La Verne College, we had a history professor. His name was Walter F. Myers, not Dr. Myers, because he did not have an advanced degree, but he knew more about history than anyone. He seemed to believe that knowledge should command ultimate respect, not three letters after your name. His appearance and demeanor were quirky, out of style with even the most sartorially lacking and behaviorally challenged academic.

He always arrived to class about three minutes late. If you were also running behind schedule you might see him roar up in his open war-surplus military jeep looking for just any place to park. He would park almost anywhere, legally or otherwise, and fly frenetically across the lawn, up the steps of Founder's Hall. For students already in their seats, the classroom door would suddenly fly open introducing a disheveled man, sloppily dressed in an ensemble of coat, tie, and pants that never matched. Pants legs were cut too short revealing socks that had lost their elastic months ago. His tousled grey hair and intense, jiggly eyes behind thick glasses made him appear as though he had just been through a violent windstorm. His scuffed, overstuffed, brown briefcase was tucked firmly under his right arm as if protecting his teaching materials from harm or pilferage. His intensity established him as someone fully ready to do something of extreme urgency.

He slammed his briefcase on the lectern and stormed across the room to fling open the same window each class period, no exceptions. He returned to the lectern and rummaged through his briefcase for the handmade charts, deadly accurate, but nearly impossible to follow. He began class as the Great Inquisitor, calling on students, alphabetically arranged, to answer questions on the voluminous list of recommended readings on reserve in the library. Every person was petrified that he would direct a question their way. No answers were ever put down or dismissed, but it was evident that you were on the right track when he put a mark after your name. You couldn't fake it with Professor Myers. His photographic memory commanded every detail of the readings.

His exams were single-spaced, testing your grasp of specific dates and events. Occasionally, you were asked to construct a detailed map of an entire region. His lectures were boring, but occasionally enlivened with personal examples. His presence at the opening of King Tut's tomb was electrifying. His home movie of the Dardanelles taken at dusk from a rowboat was a hardly discernable up and down alternation between the dark sea and a pale gray horizon. It made some people seasick. Other than that we can't recall much of the content he taught.

But there was something about Walter Myers that you couldn't quite put your finger on at the time. There was something mystical in the interplay between his encyclopedic grasp of history and his bumbling personal manner. The magic stuck with us. He touched us somewhere deep inside. He transmitted an abiding passion for human richness of the past and his example influenced our decision to become history majors. He somehow showed us that he cared. He didn't fit the conventional academic model. He was more like an iconic Mr. Chips than a standard, pedantic research historian. Lacking his doctorate, he was eventually asked to leave the college. But to us his legacy lives on. He was a great teacher.

CACOPHONY OF THEOLOGIES

Voices extolling the emotional and spiritual viewpoint of teaching are clear and consistent. They are welcome music to the ears of teachers, principals, parents, and others who care deeply about the overall well-being of young people. But given the nature of school reform policies over the years, most recently the NCLB legislation and rollout, national and state legislators are attuned to a different channel of discourse. They pay attention to aggregated data, not stories. They believe in tightening up the structure of schools and improving the technical aspects of instruction. They rely heavily on standardized numbers to measure progress on a limited set of skills. Theirs is a bird's-eye view looking at an objectified panoramic picture. This remote appraisal often overlooks the joyful and grim realities of what is going on at the grassroots level in local schools and individual classrooms. Unintended consequences often fall outside their range of view. Sometimes, the side effects are not that obvious. Just as often they're overlooked because reform policies support political agendas of presidents and governors.

But a bottom-up view often tells another story. It sees all the blemishes and messes in an up close, detailed, and intensely emotional panorama. Costs of reform are easy to calculate because they are real and personal. From the grounded view of the trenches we are paying a dear and costly price as NCLB and other efforts force us to make schools more rational and classrooms more accountable for direct results of a limited set of skills. For the first time, the law provides muscle to make sure results materialize. Change efforts also encourage a narrow conception of what it means to be a teacher. Reform policies force, as Noddings (2007) points out, "Hardworking teachers [to try] to get unwilling, unprepared students through material they have no interest in learning. Many youngsters have alternative, genuine talents, but these are disregarded" (p. 31). Neglect leads to frustration, tuning off, and dropping out the very outcomes the current legislation intends to prevent. To most teachers, making a difference means more than raising a school's aggregate performance on standardized yardsticks measuring students' academic growth.

One of the disconnects between the "other" set of books or stories and parents interested in education only for its career-enhancing value and policymakers too often concerned about their political careers is competing mind-sets about the nature of teaching. From a purely instrumental view, literature extolling the chief virtues of education as a heartfelt, soulful undertaking is seen as overly romantic, frilly new age babble. In turn, overly anxious or ambitious parents and policymakers are portrayed as hard-nosed, hyperrational, or out of touch with what students really need and the life-fulfilling role teachers play. The tug-of-war between the two theologies creates two self-sealing worlds that compete for supremacy. Policymakers control the outer fringes; classroom teachers, often surreptitiously, dominate the inner core. But for American education to make its ideal impact, legislators and parents need to consult the other set of books and teachers need to do a better job of selling the remarkable influence they wield in a young person's development. Otherwise we are headed for a hidden disaster that lies ahead, unaware of more promising alternatives.

The Miracle of Saturn

A mistaken notion that threats and tangible rewards shape behavior enjoys great currency in educational reform. The ironic working theme seems to be, "The beatings will continue until morale improves." That same mind-set governed General Motor's attitude toward its workers in the 1980s. The top-down approach almost guaranteed that people on the assembly line would mindlessly go through the motions or, even worse, creatively sabotage the quality of cars produced. Powerful unions kept wages high and working conditions reasonably predictable. The American consumers paid the price when they purchased a car. Compared to foreign imports it was a lousy, unreliable form of transportation.

Somebody at General Motors had a better idea—an automobile manufacturing plant with a soul. A representative group of workers, managers, union representatives, and others (The Gang of 99) toured the business world searching for ways to put some substantive flesh on the philosophical bones. The group distilled disparate ideas into a cohesive and unique new manufacturing way of life and Saturn was born. It was billed as "a different kind of company building a different kind of car."

Disgruntled, dispirited, and laggard GM workers were placed in a new environment of trust and cooperation. They were asked for ideas rather than ordered to conform. Teams were able to determine the way they worked. Quality became a communal watchword rather than a top-down command. Workers took pride in the cars being assembled and thought about the consumers who would ultimately drive their vehicles on the way to work, during their vacations, or while taking the kids to school. Monetary rewards were based on the performance of the company en bloc. But the intangible payoff of positive feedback from Saturn owners was of premium worth.

For a homecoming event, 44,000 Saturn owners drove to the Spring Hill plant one summer to see where their car was born and to thank the people who built it. In turn workers were able to show their gratitude for "believing in us." A line worker summed up the Saturn experience, "You know, given the chance, anyone prefers to make a perfect product. At Saturn they've given us the [opportunity], they've given us that chance. (Saturn Video–TV commercial)

Perhaps it's time for education to heed the lessons of Saturn. For decades, educational reform, with its top-down, standardized, and punitive attitude has fallen shy of expectations. Why not give schools and teachers some latitude in fixing the problems everyone agrees have become acute? The pathway to improvement will not be straight and smooth. It will be tortuous, rocky, and full of snags and disappointments. But if we assume, following the lead of Saturn, that everyone—given the chance—would like to produce a perfect outcome, we may be well advised to extend a new opportunity to educators. If a car company can have soul and automobile workers heart, why not schools and teachers? But that will only be possible if we yet again believe in teachers and they once more believe in themselves.

2

Making a Difference

The Core of Teaching

Teachers and other leaders are often held against a demanding standard: Did they make a real difference? But what does that really mean? Did the financial bottom line or test scores improve during someone's tour of duty? Or, is the difference they made a reference to something deeper and harder to put your finger on? Outcomes are typically planned and measurable. They are an important and inescapable necessity in any organization, whether a business, hospital, or school. Educational outcomes are particularly hard to pin down because schools have multiple goals. Bolman and Deal (2003) identify four such goals. Two are not typically in the forefront: custody control—keeping young people off the streets and out from underfoot; and selection and certification—channeling students into academic or vocational tracks and sorting them into colleges or careers. The third—scholastic achievement or progress toward mastering basic skills and information—is paramount and currently the focus of most of our attention. Like the first two goals, progress is quantifiable and, people believe, relatively easy to measure. The fourth—character development—is hard to quantify in the short run, and its impact may take a long time to register. But it is the goal of helping students along the road to a happy, productive life that we believe is the most significant place where teachers can make such a profound difference.

When the focus on accountability prevails over other elusive effects that bolster an enterprise's legitimacy in the eyes of its participants and publics, things begin to unravel. Rational assessment works in highly technical settings where products are concrete and verifiable. Its usefulness peters out in more amorphous situations where success is determined primarily on the basis of belief and faith.

Teachers historically have played an important role in the transmission of societal values and in the mental and moral development of children. A review of the television and film industries' portrayals of teachers over the years expresses the special place they hold for most people: *Our Miss Brooks*, *The Halls of Ivy*, *Farewell Mr. Chips*, *To Sir With Love*, *Welcome Back Kotter*, *Kindergarten Cop*, *Teachers*, *Lean on Me*, *Dead Poet's Society*, *Mr. Holland's Opus*, and *Freedom Writers* provide just a few examples. Teachers in these stories fulfill their role as dispensers of knowledge and custodians of basic skills. But they also weigh these technical duties against moral obligations as caring, inspiring role models of values, courage, faith, and hope. Tracy Kidder (1989) captures this view of teaching very poignantly when he describes a teacher's role in reconfirming and redirecting the positive life trajectory of a student whose background loomed as a handicapping road to nowhere (see Introduction). Just a soothing word, a pat on the back, or a glimmer of a hopeful tomorrow may be enough to help a young person chart a new course.

Sometimes, a teacher's impact is immediate and direct: a struggling elementary student who can all of a sudden decipher prose on the page of a book; a high school student for whom the strange symbols and equations of algebra begin to make sense; or a college student who finally "gets it" and is able to understand and apply a complex theory. Most often, these moments of insight are noticeable and provide tangible rewards for both students and teachers. Authentic "aha" experiences, ideas, and insights radiate from students. The best teachers provide stimuli that lay the groundwork for magic moments to happen. But they do not impose or force preordained ideas or concepts. Rather they conjoin pedagogy with a student's unique experiences and inner motivations. The teacher becomes a helpful guide rather than a demanding director.

SONNY AND THE BACKHOE

Ruth Ferris (1999) teaches second graders in a Copper Canyon, Texas, elementary school. Each year, she knows that she will inherit at least one student who will become her nemesis. One year it was Sonny, a bright-eyed, too-big-for-his-age bundle of unfocused energy. Sonny excelled at lunch and recess, but any attempt to center his attention on academics produced a stream of excuses and some very creative diversions. He wandered the classroom finding interesting sidetracks and actively recruiting other students in his mischievous capers. Ferris was at a loss as to how to remold her handful of pesky problems into an active, disciplined learner. His incessant meandering and recruitment efforts were starting to undermine her control of the classroom.

The breakthrough came on a bus ride to a local dramatic performance the class was to observe. While most of the children were excitedly discussing the play, Sonny was engrossed in his normal, squirrelly pursuits. Suddenly something caught his eye outside the bus window. His attention riveted on a piece of heavy equipment on a construction site: "Look Miss Ferris, there's a backhoe! And it's just like my uncle's—the one I run!"

Ferris thought about the backhoe, the toy one he had presented several times in the monthly show-and-tell sharing. Each time he brought it to school he smuggled it outside at recess to play in the dirt. Ferris was impressed by his total absorption in imaginary play. Then an idea hit her. Why not design a plan of studies for Sonny based on the backhoe? Her first effort was an illustrated story about backhoes based on a second-grade vocabulary. Sonny devoured it with rapt passion heretofore reserved for the playground and lunchtime. After pouring through the pages, he completed his written assignment in record time, one of the few pieces of work he had turned in all year. More assignments based on the backhoe received the same enthusiastic response. Sonny had taken the bait; now, it was time to set the hook.

Ferris noticed that Sonny kept all the backhoe assignments in his desk. She encouraged him to organize the material and bind it together in a book. Sonny was thrilled with the possibility. To complete the book and tie things together, he had to master his reading, writing, and other academic skills. No problem. The helter-skelter troublemaker was now as focused as a laser beam. By the year's end he had bound and published three books. Word of his accomplishments spread. Administrators, school board members, and other visitors stopped by the class to marvel at his work. Sonny took great delight in reading to them passages from his books.

The happy story hit an unexpected turn when Sonny started the third grade with a new teacher. He quickly reverted to his old behavioral patterns. At a loss as to how to handle him, his third-grade teacher consulted Ferris, who shared her pedagogical secret. With the third-grade teacher now on the right wave length, Sonny took off again, his interest having broadened to incorporate four wheelers, pickups, and other heavy equipment motivating his academic learning. Later, Sonny enrolled in a high school vocational program. His second-grade interests paved the way to a promising career and a happy life.

LEARNING FROM EXCUSES

The magic of teaching worked wonders for one second grader. But can the tailor-made approach—instead of a one-size-fits-all method—work for an inner-city high school teacher who teaches five periods of English to thirty-plus students per class? The challenge is amplified when most of the students could not care less about poetry and creative writing. They pride themselves in sticking it to their teachers, particularly those at the beginning of their career. Frank McCourt (2005) became one of those prime targets when he began his career in a New York City high school. Prior to the first day of classes, he reviewed district guidelines for preparing a lesson plan. District policy mandated a specific lesson plan—spelling out objectives and specifying activities—prior to each class. Each lesson had to produce a tangible outcome related to instructional standards, or end with a specific assignment. McCourt quickly found out that most students are not prone to follow a regimented instructional plan. They often look for any way to sabotage the effort and redirect things to suit their personal motivation of the moment. To sum it up, McCourt was getting nowhere fast.

One day, sitting at his desk while students drifted in personal reverie, a student brought McCourt a note from his mother. It persuasively proffered an excuse for an unfinished homework assignment. The problem was that the student had obviously written the note; using his left hand had failed to disguise his unique penmanship. Suddenly McCourt experienced an epiphany—a brilliant "aha" flash. He reached into his desk for the large pile of excuse notes accumulated as students labored to get themselves off the hook for work that would never materialize. He marveled at the creativity and the quality of the writing. Some notes were lengthy, others were terser:

- The toilet was blocked and we had to go down the street to the Kilkenny Bar where my cousin works to use their toilet, but that was blocked too from the night before and you can imagine how hard if was for my Ronnie to get ready for school. I hope you'll excuse him this one time and it won't happen again. The man at the Kilkenny Bar was very nice on account of how he knows your brother, [sic] Mr. McCord.

- Arnold doesn't have his work today because he was getting off the train yesterday and the door closed on his school bag and the train took it away. He yelled at the conductor who said very vulgar things as the train drove away. Something should be done.
- Her baby brother peed on her story when she was in the bathroom this morning.
- A man died in the bathroom upstairs and it over-flowed and messed up all Roberta's homework on the table. (McCourt, 2005, pp. 84–85)

McCourt suddenly realized that these kids could write—if they had something interesting to write about. That night he typed several pleas for forgiveness to distribute to his classes (minus the author's name). The next day excuses became the object of discussion. For a change, student hands were up everywhere signaling a desire to register an opinion. Following the lively exchange, McCourt gave a writing assignment: "Imagine that you have a fifteen-year-old son or daughter who needs an excuse for falling behind in English. Let it rip." Students dove into the assignment. No whining. No dawdling. Just the sound of pencils energetically putting prose to paper. They shared their creative accomplishments and asked for another assignment. McCourt wrote on the board: "Write an excuse note to God from either Adam or Eve." Again, pencils started to fly. Students skipped lunch to finish the assignment. The next day everyone had completed a creative masterpiece. Once again, the notes were shared and became the subject of a lively class discussion. In the days that followed, students wrote excuse notes for Judas, Attila the Hun, Lee Harvey Oswald, other prominent historical figures—or teachers they didn't especially like. Energy hit an all-time crescendo. A surprise visit by the district superintendent unexpectedly produced a letter of commendation rather than a stinging rebuke. McCourt now bathed in the warm joy of seeing what it meant to reap the rewards of tailoring instruction to fit the world of students.

FROM PORSCHE TO PROSE

David was a student in an alternative high school. He came from a highly educated and wealthy family but had little interest in academic work. One of the school's teachers had come to realize that motivating students was easy if you could find the right hook. One day, he pulled David from his typical half-stoned "you can't teach me squat" reverie and asked him what he wanted to do following graduation. The question caught David off guard. He seemed unusually thoughtful as he groped for an answer. Finally he blurted out, "I wanna be a Porsche mechanic." There was the hook, now to set it.

Later that afternoon, the teacher called a local Porsche mechanic, Cal, and asked if he would take David on as an apprentice. He reluctantly agreed and the next day, David was on the job. Cal fits every definition of a "good old boy" and is about as gruff and no-nonsense as they come. To say that the relationship got off to a rocky start is a profound understatement. Cal quickly figured out that David had trouble reading maintenance manuals and understanding the metric system. David asked the teacher for help because he knew that Cal was far too busy to provide remedial assistance. David worked at the Porsche shop four days a week and spent the other day at school, mastering what he had rejected before and now desperately needed to know. He became a highly motivated and focused student.

The relationship with Cal blossomed, and David came to realize he had both a real mechanical talent and also a love of working on Porsches. It looked like he had a ready-made job with Cal following graduation. But then David's parents intervened and insisted that he go to college. He reluctantly relented. To succeed in college, David would need to learn how to write. In order to graduate, the teacher insisted that he would have to submit a full-blown research paper. David dragged his feet until he hit upon a subject that interested him. He would compare the 1965 Porsche 356C with the new Porsche 911. He finished the paper in record time (Cal gave him time and material at the shop). The paper covered the problem and statistical comparison nicely. The final section reported his field testing of both cars. The 911 stood out statistically, but the 356C got the final nod based on David's clinical assessment of overall feel and driveability. A panel—the teacher and two college graduates from the community—deemed his effort suitable by higher education standards.

David graduated in June and enrolled in a state college that fall. He did well but lasted only one semester before quitting, concluding that his talent and future was in Porsches rather than academics. He is currently one of the top Porsche mechanics in Northern California, a career hatched by a teacher helping a student find a reason to learn.

Students as Candles; Teachers as Mirrors

Stories like these abound. It does not take a rocket scientist to figure out that young people will respond when learning tasks relate to their immediate experience. Miss Ferris summed it up with profound commonsense: "The learning button is always there. As teachers, we just have to identify it and gently push it" (Ferris, 1999, p. 21). Most reform legislation impels teachers to focus on prescribed skills and concepts. Meeting standards relegates motivating individual learners to a back burner. It neglects the button and undercuts the intended purposes of the mandated approach. As a consequence, many students like Sonny or McCourt's bunch fall behind and bail out. Others slog through lessons unconnected to anything they really care about. Their imaginations are dulled and their energy sapped. Their desire to learn never ignites. But to progress through the grades and reap the rewards of a diploma at the end, they have to buckle down and master what really doesn't matter much in the grander scheme of a fulfilling career and a productive life. Teachers rarely see the magic "aha" moments that result from their work with students. They too are hamstrung by the narrow focus of NCLB on uniform standards and testing. They are pressured to drum in lessons rather than to create a context which draws students into learning.

There are other ways teachers can make a difference. So much of what teachers offer students is neither planned, prompt, nor point-blank. Teachers redirect lives through subtle influence neither discernable at the time nor consciously evident until years afterward—if at all. Influence defined is "the supposed flowing of an ethereal fluid or power from the stars, thought by astrologers to affect the characters and actions of people; the power of persons or things to affect others, seen only in its effects" (*Webster's Dictionary*, 1986, p. 722). Teachers are often unaware of intangible aspects of their work typically conveyed in such simple ways as a wink, a smile, or a pat on the back. In a conversation with the vice president of a large American corporation, she put it nicely: "You'll rarely remember what teachers actually taught. But you'll never forget who they were and how they made you feel" (2004).

The mystery, magic, and majesty of teaching is overlooked by most reform legislation and torpedoed by its overwhelming emphasis on the tangible and verifiable outcomes of direct instruction. But in the memories and hearts of many students, a teacher's influence is felt and cherished for a lifetime. The awesome power of a teacher to bestow a treasured gift sets the profession apart from others. As one math teacher recalls, recognition of this magical exchange comes most often after the fact:

> *I teach math to high school sophomores. Each year, as a reward, I take the two top students from my classes to a baseball game at Dodger Stadium and pizza after the game. For the past five years, the high achievers have been students I really like; spending an evening with them is a real treat for me. This year, however, one of the kids who excelled was someone I just didn't like. I did my best not to show it, but he grated my nerves. Nonetheless, I took him to the game; he earned his ticket fair and square. But the evening was not one of my favorites. Two years later, close to graduation, the guidance counselor asked me to come to his office. As it turned out he was doing exit interviews with the seniors asking them for the lows and highs of their four years. When the counselor had asked my former student, he reached into his pocket and pulled out his ticket stub to Dodger stadium and related the time I had taken him to a game. I realized then the impact I had on students—even those I wasn't particularly fond of. (personal communication, 2001)*

Occasionally students will go to great lengths to find teachers and let them know what a difference they made. Imagine what it meant to a retired teacher to receive an e-mail from a student who remembered a magic moment of nearly thirty years ago.

> *Last month your name came up when a bunch of us were sitting around at a dinner party taking about people who permanently affected our lives. I told them about a controversial sex education course that you and another teacher taught at Sunset High School in 1968. It's taken me a long time trying to chase you down to let you know what that course meant to me. I was raped at age 12 and for 3 years after by the same man. Until your class I did not know if I was pregnant (ignorance of the times), had syphilis and might die, or if all sex was angry and violent. You brought me into reality without even knowing it,*

*allowed me to develop a healthy attitude toward "normal sex,"
and allowed me to avoid lifetime psychological problems as a
result of the rape. Many times teachers are unaware of the
impact they have on their students. I wanted you to know. (personal communication, 2007)*

Both students and teachers often have difficulty pinpoint-
ing what it is that leaves students with a lingering feeling of
affection, caring, and support. But somewhere, somehow in
the course of a school year, good feelings stick and become
cherished memories that last a lifetime:

*I taught a combination class of fourth and fifth graders many
years ago. Recently I received a call from one of the students,
now a highly successful architect in San Francisco. He wanted
me to know that he still remembers that year. He said he couldn't
put his finger on it; maybe I made him feel safe. He keeps a
picture of me and his classmates on his desk and looks at the
group portrait whenever he feels low. The class gets together
very often for a reunion. They want me to come next year. I
guess his classmates feel the same as he does—I gave them
something special. How the magic happened is still a mystery to
me. I don't care. It sure feels good to do something that matters
so much. (Martha Deal-Tubbs, personal communication,
September 9, 2007)*

Every young person needs a source of emotional and
moral support, someone who cares about and believes in
them. Families and relatives often fulfill this role. But whether
as a supportive or primary wellspring, teachers provide
essential nurturing and confidence. Very few people can look
back on school days without identifying the magic of a
teacher who cared. For Mariska Hargitay, star of television's
Law and Order SVU, Sister Margaret filled the void left by the
death of her mother, Jane Mansfield, who was killed when
Mariska was three:

She provided boundaries which children need, but there was such love . . . . I didn't know I wanted to be an actress . . . . She saw that I had talent—before I saw it myself. There's no way I'd be the actor I am without Sister Margaret. Her passion lit a fire in me. She saw me and went "you have something special"—and that made all the difference. (Bell, 2005, p. 8)

To chart a course in the complex and messy realities of growing up and leading a fruitful life as an adult, everyone needs a moral compass to point them in the right direction. When faced with troublesome and challenging situations, most of us look to role models for the right things to do or say. In their daily doings teachers, as human beacons, set examples for students. They are living icons, favorable or not, providing important lessons well beyond the scope of the official curriculum. Emulating teachers begins very early: An observation of Roberta Wright, a second-grade teacher in Austin, Texas, revealed a teacher faced with a difficult decision: what to do with a little girl who regularly was stealing classroom materials. Roberta scheduled a parent conference with the child's mother. She informed the parent of the child's misdeed and asked her if she could purchase whatever materials were lacking at home. The mother responded quickly: "Oh no, Miss Wright. Each day when she comes home, she plays like she is in school. She pretends she's you."

But the power of a teacher as a role model continues throughout life. In front of an assembled faculty at Vanderbilt University, Chancellor Joe Wyatt told the story of Roberta Wright. At the end, he paused and surveyed the several hundred faculty members in attendance. After the long moment of silence, he said with obvious conviction: "And ladies and gentlemen that doesn't end in the second grade" (Convocation speech, 2005). Message: Who you are is as important as the content you teach.

Check with anyone in a visibly important role. In peoples' rise to fame and their continued success thereafter, there will invariably be a teacher or teachers who serve as role models—positive or otherwise. First Lady Laura Bush is a good case in point. Speaking of her second-grade teacher in Midland, Texas, she said, "I wanted to be just like her when I grew up. I did become a teacher, and those experiences are among the most important of my life" (Bell, 2005, p. 8).

Thirty-five-year-old Dave Eggars is today a self-confident, best-selling author, but early in his high school days, he was an introverted adolescent with all the attending problems. He credits his turn-around to Mr. Ferry, a speech teacher:

> *His class marked the beginning of my coming out of that cocoon. There were different speeches we had to attempt, and one was the persuasive speech. Mine was about why one should take a bike trip to the mantle of the earth. I remember when I gave the speech, Mr. Ferry never blinked an eye . . . with Mr. Ferry there was never a sense that my work wasn't appropriate or weighty enough. (After his class I started writing for the newspaper and literary magazines.) Sometimes a good teacher can be the person who sets you on a course. (Bell, 2005, p. 8)*

SORTING OUT WHAT REALLY MATTERS

In casting a net to capture the outcomes of education, reform initiatives typically overly rely on a wide gauge of mesh which captures only results that are easy to measure. Other important lessons students may learn from instruction, from examples teachers set, or from feelings about themselves that last a lifetime, pass through the net unrecognized. They are lost, largely irretrievable, even though these outcomes are far more valuable than the retention of concrete information assessed through standardized testing.

Many today downplay the spiritual aspects of teaching as idealistic or overly romantic. But where else is an impassioned modus operandi needed more? Teaching is a calling, a virtuous profession that leaves its mark on the most hopeful promises for a better future—our young people. To the extent that the overly rational, decidedly technical emphasis of NCLB shackles the core efforts of teachers, the stewards of hope, we are moving sideways rather than progressing ahead. The delicate balance between tangible outcomes and subtle influences has tipped and we need to reinvigorate the heart and soul of teaching.

3

School Reform
A Ground Level Perspective

From a policy perspective, educational reform is vital to the nation's health and welfare. From their remote and detached positions, policymakers are perplexed by the seeming recalcitrance of local educators to carry out legislated mandates. But for local administrators and teachers, especially those who have been around for a long time, the situation looks very different. They have witnessed a carousel of reforms that seem endless. A few of these past reforms that have flared up and faded away include individualized instruction, the new math, whole word reading, whole language, team-teaching, open space architecture, teacher-proof curricula, PPBS (teaching to objectives), differentiated staffing, parental choice, accountability, merit-pay, TQM, and differentiated salaries. Most of these initiatives died out, while some lingered on and others were repackaged and tried again.

THE PARADOX OF CHANGE

This fascination with change (now a noun as well as a verb) is not confined to schools. In a debate during the presidential campaign of 2007, the noun change was invoked over fifty times. Each candidate postured him- or herself as the prime agent of change. Other sectors face similar pressures to cast off the old for something new. A conference of management and leadership scholars who convened at the Harvard Graduate School of Education reached the following conclusion about change efforts: First, you try it in business. If it doesn't pan out, you give it a whirl in healthcare. If it fizzles, try higher education. If no luck there, foist it on local schools. As a last chance, export it to developing countries. As a backup, give the initiative another name and recycle. The truth is Americans welcome change only as long as they personally don't have to do anything differently.

Set in this historical context, No Child Left Behind (NCLB) is the continuation of educational reforms given a boost by the highly influential *A Nation at Risk* report over twenty years ago. Most of these past endeavors have failed to live up to the expectations of sponsors. In too many instances they have caused extensive harm and dampened people's faith in public schools. The recent legislation is meant to assure that all children in America's schools, especially minority or economically disadvantaged students, have a shot at a solid grounding in basic reading and computational skills. But lurking behind the cloak of goodness are some troublesome realities. Like previous school improvement legislation, the law relies almost exclusively on standardized testing to measure progress, this time establishing "adequate yearly progress" (AYP) as the key outcome. The dominant mode to assure compliance leans heavily toward a "stick" versus a "carrot" mentality. Low-performing schools incur significant sanctions if they fail to measure up on a truncated timeline. In California, this includes state-sponsored teams of coaches who try to help. Usually, these consultants are seen as a mixed blessing by those being coached. "Frills" such as the arts, field trips, or even recess often fall outside the scope of what schools should be about. There is concern among many liberals that NCLB is really a conspiracy on the part of conservatives to pave the way for the privatization of schools.

Past the rhetoric, public controversy, and questionable intentions, formal assessments of NCLB's impact are revealing some noteworthy costs, including disproportionate failures of lower class and minority schools to meet the standards bringing on penalties and increasing dropout rates. Carl Cohn (2007), superintendent of San Diego schools, writes,

> *If one of my district's schools misses just one of 19 federally mandated goals, I must label it a failing school. Once this school is labeled a failure, I am required to sanction it. These sanctions include offering untested private schooling to all students, regardless of their performance or whether the services have any benefit; busing students to other schools, regardless of whether those schools are better; and closing, restructuring the school into a charter school, regardless of whether that process will improve it.*

Most public assessments of change efforts, such as NCLB, are once removed accounts that objectify the problems and skew positive results. On the floor level, views of parents, teachers, and students cast even more doubt on how well the legislation is really panning out. Their perspective is personal, emotional, and extremely disturbing. Every student, teacher, and parent has a name, and many of their lives are turned topsy-turvy by NCLB, its attendant emphasis on standardized testing, and its chokehold on a constricted view of the purpose of education.

TEACHERS' OUTLOOKS

Teaching is both an art and a science. Good teaching is a balance between the two. NCLB undercuts a teacher's discretion and creativity. As a result, teaching has become more mechanical than magical. Short-term standardization has drowned out enduring lessons from the heart. The full range of what a teacher can offer to a student has been severely squelched.

The kindergarten teacher, a child's first exposure to the public school, works with students in a wide range of development. Some students come from homes with a plethora of books and a strong belief in the importance of literacy. Others have rarely, if ever, read a book or been read to. These literary-deprived children come to school where the teacher introduces them to the power of learning. A longtime kindergarten teacher shares her frustration in the following:

> *I teach kindergarten. In my 15 years, I have retained one child. This year, I retained seven. It's all because of this insanity surrounding NCLB. My judgment doesn't seem to matter anymore. I know that these kids are now stamped REJECT. I'm afraid that will follow them as they progress through the grades. But, what can I do? Someone else is pulling the strings. I'm just a teacher.*

Tracking students is often viewed as a form of discrimination in the schools. Better, more experienced teachers are used in classrooms for the privileged, while at-risk students struggle in lesser facilities with novice teachers who try but often fall short. In the world of NCLB, a new form of tracking has been discovered and renamed. We now have the "bubble kids."

Several years ago, New York City launched a new accountability program for garbage workers. Instead of being paid by the hour, employees were now compensated for the amount of refuse they picked up. Soon after the new system was put into place, workers figured out that if they watered their load before weigh-in, the size of their paycheck would increase. In the case of NCLB and other accountability systems, teachers' salaries don't change when test scores rise or fall. But their reputations as good teachers or their schools' reputations are tied to "data-driven" results. Making a difference has been redefined numerically by how well students perform on standardized tests.

In a Texas elementary school, teachers soon figured out how to buck the official system. They established a form of "triage." Students are sorted into three categories based on their reading test scores: safe, suitable, or hopeless. Those just below the cutoff level of 70 (60–69) are labeled as "bubble kids" who, with some extra attention, could achieve a passing score. "Nonurgent" or "remedial" students are shunted to the side or placed in special programs. Moving students from nonpassing to passing assures a teacher's reputation as well as the school's appearance as a "good school." Plaudits and other rewards are given to high-scoring schools. Those with lower results are penalized. If this practice was an exception, it would raise several issues. But, even worse, it's becoming the norm.

In a California middle school, "bubble kids" are provided with two periods a week of intensive study to bring them over the line. Students are pulled out of their regular science class twice a week for one-on-one tutoring. While this may achieve the desired results, a higher number of students who bolster the school's AYP numbers, what about the student who is below basic and really needs the help? These students are ignored, as they are considered beyond help. On the other end of the spectrum, the high achievers are also brushed aside; they already score high enough and can fend for themselves.

The drill and kill focus on standardized tests makes the classroom a lockstep, sterile place to be. In her new book *Tested*, Linda Perlstein (2007) reports her observations in an Annapolis, Maryland, classroom:

Teachers were held to scripted curricula, required to make academic progress every day. On Day 1, first graders were drilled on the difference between consonants and vowels. Independent reading and rich imaginative play were out the window. In this version of schooling, students don't simply respond to a piece of writing. They must learn (in third grade) to create a "brief constructed response"—which has an acronym (like everything else), BCR. Students are taught to use BATS, to Borrow from the question, Answer the question, use Text support and Stretch. These students must do five BCRs per day, in their practice for March testing days. They must also answer the question, "Why is this a poem?" With such inane (and wrong) comments as, "I know it is a poem because it rhymes and has stanzas." Don't tell Allen Ginsberg. Stories are reduced to the "message"—devoid of wonder. (p. 87)

Even the ceremonial side of learning has been co-opted by the test-oriented, behaviorist approach. At Thanksgiving, turkey decorations reflect classroom standards. "We are thankful for great behavior!" If this mind-set dominates more than one classroom in this country, the magic of teaching is in jeopardy.

HUMAN TOUCH: THE ENDANGERED INGREDIENT

Try a thought experiment. Think of a teacher who was significant in your life. Was he or she wedded to specific standards and high-stakes tests? As you visualize this teacher who made a difference, a warm yet demanding personality, fairness, and interesting new vistas are usually part of the schema. In many teacher education programs, prospective candidates are asked to reflect on good teachers in their lives and talk about what made them great. Without exception the responses include answers like the following:

"They cared."

"They took time for me."

"Creativity was a part of every lesson."

"They challenged us."

"She believed in me, that I could do anything."

"He saw what I needed and jump-started my excitement about school and life."

"They were always available, after school, during recess."

"I was never afraid to ask questions, no matter how dumb they sounded."

"They made learning fun."

Tyack and Cuban (1995) report a parallel reaction when they ask people in civic groups to recall favorable memories of their student days in public schools:

On occasion, in talking about school reform with civic groups, we have asked people to recall their best experiences as students in public schools. Almost always, they remember the influence of a teacher who challenged them to develop their potential, who made a subject come alive, or who gave caring advice at a stressful time. (p. 136)

In today's world, it is difficult for teachers to find time to add the human touch. The emphasis is on "research-based" education and making sure everything is "measurable." After state testing is complete, teachers feel free to sponsor activities that make for enduring school memories. A colleague takes his AP history class and prepares and presents a Rogers and Hammerstein musical. Accompanied by a CD, students take their parts and sing along with the professionals. Students begin by saying, "We don't want anyone to see this performance." This is followed by, "Can we have costumes?" And finally, "Can we have it in the Student Center and invite our friends?" The pure joy of putting on these yearly productions creates the space to incubate memorable moments that are not easily forgotten.

Following spring testing, elementary school teachers joyfully launch their integrated thematic units. Students build things, write plays, and turn the room into a rain forest—all activities destined to become part of a student's cherished recollection of school. Remember how much a creative "with-it" teacher meant to you. It was dismal when a substitute took his or her place in the classroom. Today's pressures for quantifiable results produce aggravation among teachers, and a frustration about the lack of time to do the unstructured activities that really make a difference.

In middle schools, English classes on the second and third day of the school year are set aside for diagnostic tests. This practice does not give the teacher the opportunity to begin to develop a relationship with students or to promote a cohesive group identity for the class. To add fuel to the fire, teachers have to take two additional days away from the classroom to assess the tests. Over a month during the school year is used for state and district tests. It makes the teachers ask, "When is there time to teach the students what they need to learn for the tests?" The other lament is the lack of time to teach students to think critically. Teachers are so pressured to ensure that students will master the facts that there is little time left for collaborative activities that promote critical and creative thinking to help the students figure out what the facts really mean. Some teachers slip around the barriers to address basic emotional needs.

JANET HART'S TOUCH

Janet Hart, a kindergarten teacher in California, was struggling with a student who was having a difficult time adjusting to class expectations. For the first two weeks of school, Araceli stayed at the back of the room sobbing. The first week the weeping was loud and disruptive. By the second week it had subsided to a quiet whimper. Fortunately, Ms. Hart had fifteen years of experience behind her so she understood separation anxiety. She quietly and patiently encouraged the child to move a little closer to the other students. Tentatively, the little girl began to join in at a minimal level. By the time the first month ended, Araceli was a full participant in class, obviously feeling a welcomed acceptance. But, as often happens today, her family moved during the third month of school. About a month after the move Ms. Hart received a call from a teacher in another school district. She said she was Araceli's new teacher, and could not get her to take part in classroom activities. Araceli stayed by the door and wailed every day. She asked Ms. Hart what strategies she used to help the child participate. Ms. Hart explained how she had slowly encouraged her to join in, a little each day, until she felt comfortable with other students. The new teacher paused, and then said, "Oh, I don't have time for that. We have to work on the standards, not baby students."

Missing the Boat

Accountability and assessment are a necessary part of education. In order to improve, any organization needs to ferret out what it is working and what needs attention. The question is where to focus attention and how immediate or far in the future data should be gathered. It is when short-term functions take precedence over the real job of teaching and learning that the train derails. Does one test in a single point of time prove high schools are doing the job? Our high schools are caught up in this unrelenting drive to prove their success at the moment. In many states the High School Exit Exam is a compulsive reality, along with an increased emphasis on advanced placement and honors programs. Students who are academically adequate but not gifted are often left to fend for themselves and depress a school's composite score. But what about those who are inspired by their teachers and later blossom? Balancing lessons from the fable *The Tortoise and the Hare* may be an important complement to the current real-time snapshot. Jack Welch, legendary CEO of GE, offered some sage advice for policymakers and educational leaders: "You can't grow long term if you can't eat short term. Anybody can manage short. Anybody can manage long. Balancing those two things is what management is."

Myopic vision often produces nonsensical outcomes. One large high school has a club for students who want to volunteer in local agencies. The concept provides a wonderful opportunity to place students in real situations to work alongside experienced professionals. These students are interested in pursuing the value of service as a part of their adult careers. One college-bound student, not enrolled in either advanced placement or honors programs, asked to join the service-oriented club. She was refused because she was not taking the appropriate classes. This is an indefensible exclusion of the worst kind; a segregation born out of the need to prove a school's in vogue reputation while downplaying the future prospects of its students.

Think of a book you read that made you realize there was an exciting, opulent world out there to be discovered and explored. For some it may be *Little Women*, for others *To Kill a Mockingbird*, or maybe for you it was *The Giver*. It doesn't matter when it happened; what matters is that it heightened your imagination and curiosity.

Educators have long recognized that reading is the launching pad for subsequent learning. Without the ability to read, a student is doomed to a life of mediocrity. But how can we assess a student's ability to read? Is standardized testing the only measure? Anyone sitting in front of an individual student reading aloud can determine how well he or she reads. Exactly what the problem may be also stands out in a face-to-face diagnosis.

Most of the standardized instruments aggregate data by groups. They have little diagnostic value. They also are plagued with cultural and linguistic bias. Scripted whole class reading programs are not only repetitive and joyless, they also introduce words and phrases that have different cultural meanings. In one reading series, Nan is an important decodable word. Yet, in the same group of stories Nan is also a baby, an older girl playing baseball, and a cat. This is particularly troublesome in a state like California where large numbers of students have Spanish as a first language. Names like Sam, Nan, Fan, and Pat abound. These are not names that are often recognizable by students from different linguistic traditions. But, under the jurisdiction of NCLB, teachers are rarely given the latitude to alter what is being taught. For example, a kindergarten teacher was working with a child on a story titled *One Big Fat Fig.* "Sim can find a big fat fig. Can Sim hit the big fig? Sim ran. Sim hit the big fig. Sim bit the big fat fig" (Weeks, 2003, pp. 37–40). When the child finished reading the story he asked the teacher, "What is a Sim?" While students may learn to decode words and score well on tests, where is the path to fluency and comprehension that brings joy to the critical skill of reading for all students?

Taken together, mandated teacher responses to top-down reform have often tipped the balance, gutting schools of their meaning and purpose. Too much focus is placed on things that really don't matter such as time-bound information or rote skills that turn teachers into shackled technicians hobbled from exercising professional discretion. It makes for unhappy teachers, unimaginative students, and sterile or toxic schools. Over time these costs may come back to haunt us by producing students without imagination who are unable to think creatively or critically. We also run the risk of losing some of our most talented teachers.

PARENTS' APPREHENSION

Many parents do not understand the rationale behind NCLB and the heightened emphasis on testing. Others half-heartedly buy in, seduced in part by the reform's public rhetoric that schools need to be held accountable for how well students learn. They want what's best for their offspring and because of the constant widespread criticism of public education, they worry about the quality of instruction at their local schools. They are looking for reassurance, but their fears loom large. A parent commented:

Recently my children's elementary school failed to meet adequate yearly progress for a particular minority's reading progress under the No Child Left Behind Act and was placed on a warning list. This meant parents might gain the right to transfer their children to another school in the district. Never mind that this very same school sent more kids to the district's gifted program than any other, or that this entire district has the highest SAT scores of any district in the state. The day the news broke six different moms (none in the affected minority) asked me if I was going to transfer my kids. From neighborhood pride and joy to threat to a child's future overnight.

Most parents want their young charges to be happy and well rounded. Many are worried about the personal shortfalls of standardization and testing. For example, a custodian in a large California school district was troubled over his two daughters' reaction to school:

My kids used to love going to school. They would get up early in the morning, excited about what learning the day would produce. Now, it's hard to get them out of bed in the morning. They hate school. My younger daughter throws up every morning before she goes to school, particularly on testing days, which are too plentiful. I don't know what to do.

A student has to want to learn in order to move ahead. When parents see that desire ebbing away, they become anxious and fearful for their children's well-being:

My son used to worship his teachers. He felt they cared about him and were an advocate for his learning progress. Now he sees his teachers as protagonists who have lost their love for teaching and learning. He's a good kid and has, up until now, achieved at above satisfactory levels. At a recent parent conference I asked the teacher how someone who passed the high school exit exam at the beginning of his sophomore year with high scores in English could be struggling in his English class this year. Her response: "His performance may have been adequate then, but that's when the bar was set lower. Today we have higher expectations and your son is not measuring up."

My seven-year-old son is one of the most imaginative, creative kids I've ever seen, and it's not just because I'm his mother.

*He used to love going to school and was hungry and would gob-
ble up new ideas as if they were chocolate candy. He now comes
home from school crying and says, "Mom it's just so hard and
boring. All we do is take tests."*

Why is it the more we know about learning, the less attention we pay to what really works? We talk about "research-
based" practices, yet many actions in the classroom are polar
opposites. Heath and Heath (2007) label this the "Curse of
Knowledge," when our book learning mutes our commonsense wisdom and makes it hard to communicate with others
"not in the know."

A first-grade teacher was working with a group of parents
helping them understand the latest brain research on learning.
The group was watching a DVD featuring the work of Marian
Diamond, Pat Wolff, and Eric Jenson. It highlighted the
importance of a variety of approaches for effective teaching,
including hands-on activities. One of the mothers in the group
commented to the teacher, "When my other daughter was in
first grade those were the strategies used. She loved them, and
she learned. Why don't they teach that way anymore?"

While many parents may feel comforted by the rhetorical
assurances of NCLB, others feel helpless in dealing with their
own children for whom school has now become a disquieting
albatross that makes going to school a chore rather than a joy.

STUDENT QUALMS

The primary intention of the high-stakes testing of NCLB was
to assure that all students receive appropriate instruction. To a
certain extent, measures of performance did let students know
where they stood in relation to others. The problem is that
those who score poorly time and again become frustrated and
are made to feel like they are worthless. Their primary reaction is very often to either tune out or drop out. Students
whose scores are exemplary often become bored, yearning for

activities that will stretch their core interests and concerns. Some even purposely try not to do well just because they can.

> *A second-grade boy was talking about the big tests that were to begin that day. It was evident his teacher had impressed on him the importance of THE TEST. The conversation continued, and he shared that he had a big game that afternoon. His team, the Nationals, was playing the Orioles. Both teams had only one loss making it a very important game. Out of curiosity, I asked, "Which is more important, your test or your game with the Orioles?" He looked at me like I was crazy and replied, "The game with the Orioles of course." Even as a second grader, he had his priorities straight.*

In the narrow pursuit of results, young people are often the casualties. Fear has no place in daily school life, just as Deming (1986) advocated, and driving it out of the workplace is a first step in producing high-quality goods and services. Yet fear in today's schools erects a formidable, ever-present barrier to first-rate teaching and learning.

> *A seasoned public school teacher was talking with her seven-year-old granddaughter about school. She's in the second grade, the first year testing begins in earnest in her district and she was talking about her test-taking experiences. "Grandma, guess what happens if I don't fill in the bubbles on the test." "What?" "The test police will get me!"*

How does this environment affect a marginalized high school student?

> *I wasn't left behind. I just realized I wasn't getting ahead. All I did, it seems, was take tests that may have been important to somebody. To me it was a bunch of bullshit that I would never use. I joined a gang and learned the lit in three days. I'm not dumb. I just wasn't turned on, so I tuned out and dropped out. In a gang I'm somebody, not somebody that nobody knows.*

They say a picture is worth a thousand words. When tenth-grade students were asked to draw their feelings on test day, some interesting results came out. The focus was to assess where tenth-grade students are emotionally in relationship to high-stakes testing. Each student was asked to draw how he or she feels when confronted with an important test. The drawings were dramatic in what they revealed. Less than twenty percent of them were positive, many were neutral, but a high percentage represented highly anxious feelings. Students marginalized themselves, in many cases showing themselves as a small drawing covering a tiny percentage of the page. Feelings of isolation were frequently represented. Perhaps the most powerful outcome was the part adults played in the drawings. Not one single positive picture of an adult came out of the study. Some drawings showed the teacher with a whip, while others pictured the teacher laughing at the students. Perhaps the saddest depiction was that of an adult with a gun, holding it over the student.

RECALIBRATING NCLB

Accumulating evidence shows that higher standards and tighter accountability are not having their intended impact. Reform focuses on a narrow band of instructional goals and overlooks critical thinking, creativity, imagination, emotional intelligence, and joy. Rather than preparing active civic-minded adults for meaningful and productive lives, the program emphasizes facts that will soon be obsolete. It touts the importance of objectivity and certainty while ignoring the fact that most of the challenges students will face are subjective and difficult to pin down. Once again, there is a need for better balance.

NCLB has undoubtedly had some impact by increasing awareness of learning outcomes for all students, especially in schools where apathy, negativity, and hopelessness have undercut teachers' sense of efficacy and students' desire to learn. But in accomplishing these positive changes, the central core of teaching and learning has too often been sacrificed. The delicate balance between academic progress and character development has been tipped too far in the direction of standards and measurement. Restoring equilibrium will require a revival of the historically grounded, existential basics of what public schools are really about: making a difference in the quality of life and recognizing the promise of potential. This will liberate talented teachers to be who they really are rather than what policymakers would like them to become.

4

Being Real

The Authentic Teacher

Students can quickly spot teachers who are bogus. The transparent gap between their words and deeds tells the real story. They hide behind their bureaucratic authority not realizing that their efforts to keep control masks who they really are and undermines their moral authority as teachers. Students see through this charade well enough to pinpoint the inconsistency and then respond in kind. They can make the classroom a real hell on earth—especially for new teachers who are coached not to smile until Christmas. A college professor of education warned Frank McCourt (2005) about his first days as a new teacher: "The way you meet and greet your first class might determine the course of your whole career. Your whole career. They're watching you. You're watching them. You're dealing with American teenagers, a dangerous species, and they'll show you no mercy" (p. 39).

With a warning like that, it is no wonder that a beginning teacher, or an experienced teacher greeting a new class, feels tempted to hang up his or her humanity outside the classroom and don a suit of protective armor. To expose yourself would invite losing control. And, deep down, that fear haunts every teacher. Give students an inch and they will take a mile. Better to let them know who is boss from the beginning. The problem is that the defensive shield forecloses any chance to develop a genuine relationship with a class or individual students. Students quickly ferret out a farce:

> *You can fool some of the kids some of the time, but they know when you are wearing the mask, and you know they know. They force you into truth. If you contradict yourself they'll call out, "Hey, that's not what you said last week." You face years of experience and their collective truth, and if you insist on hiding behind the teacher mask you lose them. Even if they lie to themselves and the world they look for honesty in the teacher. (p. 203)*

THE PATCHWORK OF TEACHING

A teacher is more than a formal role and teaching well requires sharing your true self. Authenticity, genuineness— being real—begins with a bedrock sense of who you are and what you hold most dear. Parker Palmer (1998) writes about the importance of self-knowledge:

> *They do not care what graduate school you attended, who chaired your committee, or how many books you have written, but they quickly sense whether you are real and they respond accordingly. The discerning innocence of young children deepens my conviction that at every level of education, the selfhood of the teacher is the key. (p. 7)*

There is no "one-size-fits-all" approach to good teaching. A school is like a quilt sewn of many unique classrooms. Some teachers talk a lot while students await lessons to unfold. Others draw out students, thinking understanding will emerge from a spirited dialogue. Some teachers are strict and demand that students toe the line. Others are convinced that freedom encourages students to explore and learn from experience. The secret of grooming the young derives from the authenticity or genuineness of the teacher. Once more quoting Palmer (1998), "Good teachers share one trait: a strong sense of personal identity infuses their work" (p. 10).

Consider the example of two memorable teachers now deceased, Miss Anne Juhl and Mr. George Savo. The two are polar opposites in almost every respect.

Miss Juhl

Miss Juhl was the modern embodiment of the iconic French character, the *institutrice* or school mistress. She had a flair for the dramatic in both her dress and demeanor. She was a tall, stately woman with a magnificent mane of gray hair. Cloaked in her knitted cape atop a colorful dress, she would swirl into the faculty lounge commanding an aura of respect that her colleagues could not equal, and even trumped the authority of the school's principal. There was no doubt to anyone that she ruled the roost in her classroom and was also a formidable force to be reckoned with in both the school and the surrounding community. Students would do anything to escape her wrath—especially completing assignments on time according to strict specifications.

Mr. Savo

Mr. Savo was almost the mirror image of Miss Juhl. While she taught in a tough inner city junior high school, he was a high school teacher in an affluent, artsy beach community. Mr. Savo was a classic long-time bohemian beatnik. His gray-flecked beard, tousled head of hair, and weathered face gave testimony to his seasoned years of wisdom. He lived with his internationally recognized artist wife in a sparsely furnished home in which any counterculture hippie would feel at home. He baked his own bread and grew organic vegetables. His rumpled, faded blue jeans, open-at-the-neck blue denim work shirt, and Birkenstock sandals worn both at home and at school signaled that he was as laid back as they come.

All of Mr. Savo's social studies classes relied on the give-and-take Socratic dialogue approach. Topics for discussion reflected whatever happened to be on students' minds on a particular day. His loose, informal style would gently nudge the discussion toward an appropriate focus. But it was very clear that the students, in tandem with the teacher, shaped the curriculum. Any directives from above about what to teach quickly disappeared in the spirited and buoyant verbal exchange between teacher and students or among students themselves. Mr. Savo's style embodied the values of the 1970s counterculture. But it was clear that he was on an alternative frequency long before it was in vogue.

Yin and Yang

Both teachers, in their own ways, made a lasting imprint on their students. Testimony from past students affirms each teacher's unique character and lasting influence. A former student relates her memories of Miss Juhl:

She was an imposing person. She was always immaculately dressed, a beautiful woman with a gorgeous head of hair. On a rainy day, she would come into the room with a plastic bag over her hair and with plastic bags on her shoes in place of rain boots. Miss Juhl was knowledgeable and had an amazing vocabulary. She had a flair for the dramatic. She knew so much about every-thing. I remember her talking a lot. You never talked when she was talking. She was strict. She made us think. With Miss Juhl, you knew you had to learn, but she also made you want to find out. Sometimes, I think she even shocked people into learning. One thing for sure, we remembered what we learned in her class. And we will always remember Miss Juhl. No one ever for-got her. When I was in high school, several of us were riding our bikes on the wrong side of the street. A police officer pulled us over and was about to give us a ticket. I told him that my teacher, Miss Juhl, said it was correct to ride on the other side of the street. He looked at me and said, "I had Miss Juhl and she was rarely wrong. I'll let you go with a warning. But you need to move to the other side of the street."

A former student shares his recollections about Mr. Savo:

From what I can remember Mr. Savo was a man who was very disciplined yet at the same time kind and understanding. He would at times let his emotions loose and let you know that he was serious about whatever the topic was about. I remember him telling me (in his stern, heavy Yugoslavian tone), "Ralph, you should take things more seriously. I know you can achieve whatever you want as long as you focus on what you want." He always had great words of wisdom. I remember him getting mad at me once for flirting with this gal during a movie we were watching. Shame on me! I also was one of his students he trained in fencing. He seemed to truly love the sport and was quite good at it. He carried out his laid-back discipline in all aspects of what he did. Although at times I would fear him, I always respected and cared about him. Even though what I have said about him sounds more like he was a serious person, he also had a very good sense of humor. He would every now and then tell a joke in class and he would be the one falling apart first! Above all else, George was a good man!

THE INNER PATH

Beginning teachers in college and university programs emphasize techniques—the "how to" of classroom instruction. This overlooks the essential core of teaching, the inner world of the teacher. It's hard to be real when you don't know your self, your own unique identity. McCourt (2005) underscores the point: "You have to make your own way in the classroom. You have to find yourself. You have to develop your own style, your own techniques. You have to tell the truth or you'll be found out" (p. 113).

Authenticity cuts deeply into the psyche below the intellect. It centers on two often overlooked features of being human—heart and soul. It has been said that the heart has a mind of its own. Heart gives us the courage to buck the tide when we are true to our most ardent inclinations. To be faint of heart causes us to waffle when the going gets tough. Soul, related to heart, is a repository of the profound and sacred ideals that we hold most dear. Our very essence resides in the inmost recesses of our soul. It is the moral compass that guides us in the right direction and gives life buoyancy and zest.

The path to discovering our hearts and souls is an inner journey. It requires us to entertain some penetrating existential questions: "Who am I?" "Where did I come from?" "Where am I headed?" "What are my cardinal values and beliefs?" "What principles would I be willing to go to jail to protect?" "If the need arises, what am I willing to die for?" "What would people miss most if I was gone?" These questions take you to the nub of who you really are, expose your unique identity, and reveal what you are willing to risk to uphold your integrity.

Both Miss Juhl and Mr. Savo were heartfelt and soulful teachers. They knew who they were and their purpose in teaching. Both obviously would go to the mat to defend their beliefs and justify their demeanor. Their students could sense their integrity and open their minds, hearts, and souls to the lessons both had to offer. As a result their teachings stuck and provided lifelong inspiration and direction to their students.

Ideally, teachers' work is imbued with a deep sense of moral purpose, a calling. Some teachers view teaching as a job, time spent in a classroom in exchange for pay. Work, on the other hand, is different.

Work comes from inside out; work is the expression of our soul, of our inner being. It is unique to the individual; it is creative.

Work is an expression of the spirit at work in a world through us. Work is that which puts us in touch with others, not so much at the level of personal interaction, but at the level of service in the community. (Fox, 1995, p. 5)

The true joy of teaching comes from the unique ability of teachers to influence young people by drawing out and nurturing what they have inside and encouraging them to forge ahead and blaze their own unique paths. The narrowing of accountability to a restricted range of calculable outcomes eats away at this noble, definitive purpose of the profession: "For 'called' teachers, facing threatening accountability measures puts the entire self at risk" (Bullough, 2006, p. 8).

Imagine what it's like for an accomplished craftsperson, accustomed to putting a signature on inspired work, to be given a job on an assembly line where he or she is a cog in a machine that produces someone else's product. Each year, teachers receive a fresh set of new faces, a new batch of promises awaiting fulfillment. In Georgia, parents met with the school principal to arrange the transfer of their third-grader to another school in the district because they had recently moved to a new attendance zone. The principal sent an aide to fetch the boy. The aide returned with a message from Mrs. Gustafson, the third-grade teacher, which said, "You can't have him. I'm not through with him yet." With smiles on their faces, the principal and the parents worked out an arrangement for the student to continue until the end of the school year. That kind of dedication is being usurped by standardized curricula and tests that exist independent of the teacher's professional judgment.

Reform prods an authentic teacher into an existential quandary: Do I teach the way my heart and soul tell me is right, or do I buckle under pressure and teach to the imposed standards and mandated tests? Taking the self-defined right path entails obvious external risks, but caving in to forces that go against one's genuine personal grain undermines the moral sway of a true teacher.

The Sultan of Spunk

Laura Deal-Russi, a teacher at a Southern California school, epitomizes the authentic teacher who puts what she thinks is right for her students above the dictates of NCLB. Mrs. Deal-Russi has taught for twenty years in the same school. Although she is a seasoned veteran, her youthful appearance might lead you to conclude that she is a beginning teacher. Her elementary school, the oldest in the district, serves a low-income student population, primarily White and Hispanic. Her classroom is home to twenty first graders.

From the get-go, it is obvious that Deal-Russi is passionate about her work. Her chief objective is to make learning interesting, to hook students so that they become self-motivated. Early on in her career she consulted the district curriculum guide, which to her seemed not only dull and poorly presented, but also leading her down a path quite different than the one she wanted to follow. The guide was teacher-centered and she wanted to inspire students to explore:

The way I teach is a personality thing. We start the day with everyone sitting on a rug—including me. I want to get a buzz going so students get excited about what they are learning. We write about everything we do. I want them to really understand what they are learning. I want them to see interconnections among lessons, to weave the ideas into their everyday lives. Students do oral reports to share their learning with others. Dittoes aren't for me. Answering prepackaged written assignments deadens their imagination. I want them to question things—always asking, "Why"? I want kids to get stoked up. If we're doing a unit on skeletons, we don't start with definitions or labels. I bring in some bones. That peaks their curiosity and motivates them to put things together in their own way, in their language. You can learn a lot from bones rather than me telling them what they need to know.

Deal-Russi's principal puts a strong emphasis on research-based, data-driven teaching practices. To her, the standards provide something to fall back on when your experience leaves some gaps. But to be wed solely to standards creates compliant people who can't risk being different. Following the rules may be safe but too often deflects attention from those vital "teaching moments" when learning becomes particularly meaningful. For example, Deal-Russi stresses the importance of reading skills but tries to get students excited about what they are reading. To her, desire is the driving force in learning to read. She consistently checks student progress by having them read to her and then discuss what a passage or page means. Very often, she finds that competent readers don't score well on standardized tests. She attributes this to a lack of interest in testing. Some students score well but are indifferent to how reading relates to their lives.

Deal-Russi is not at all shy about defending her experience-derived approach to instruction:

> I believe in what I'm doing because I know firsthand that it works. If I'm pressured to do something else, I'll go underground. I can defend what I do to anyone. For example, on Halloween we fuse witches, ghosts, and other supernatural figures to get them excited about reading and writing. Some parents complained about our endorsement of Pagan images. We stood our ground and wrote a justification for what we were doing and why. That satisfied the parents, who then backed down. Look, I know what I'm doing. I'm not going to let new unfounded ideas bulldoze mine. I'll never go down without a fight. I'm not going to waste kids' time with what I know doesn't work.

In response to parents' complaints about the Halloween activity of constructing Apple Witches, Deal-Russi and her colleagues responded in a nondefensive, constructive way. They wrote a letter detailing how the activity incorporated the school district's instructional objectives for the first grade.

They altered the assignment for students whose parents objected to witches. These students constructed an old lady instead. Excitement generated by the project engages students intensively and joyfully in learning without specifically defining the underlying instructional outcomes. For students, it's a playful activity. For teachers, it is a highly effective means to accomplish important instructional ends.

With Deal-Russi, what you see is what you get. She's the same both on and off duty. There is no stage face for different scenes. Her friends and relatives see the same person the students see in her classroom:

> *I believe in saying things straightforward. People know when you're talking in Morse code. Even little kids know when you're faking it. They are never surprised in what I do and respond when I tell them this is how it's going to go. They know they're going to get nailed if they misbehave. There needs to be a balance between being touchy feely and being rigid. Kids know that in the middle zone they and I can "play ping-pong." We just don't cross over the line. My kids think I'm a regular person. They are part of my life.*

FINDING YOUR GENUINENESS

Authenticity and being real goes a long way in the work of teaching. It's not something you learn in teacher education classes. It's something you learn in life through trial and error. The beauty of it is that everyone takes different lessons from experience. For the teaching profession, that means that teachers come in all shapes and sizes—as it should be. Being true to one's self is a prime requisite for good teaching. Trying to cast teachers from the same mold or standardizing how they teach is an effort of extreme futility. Good teaching provides students with lasting lessons and encourages them to lead productive and meaningful lives. Memories as well as mechanics shape students who know who they are and what they might become while also helping them master basic, technical skills. Helping young people know and appreciate their individual gifts is far superior to trying to elbow them into a predetermined profile. Only teachers true to themselves have the genuine talents to make this happen. Unfortunately, there is no recipe for how to become authentic. Teachers have to find their own way. If you follow the main road, you will most likely arrive at your destination; if you follow your heart, you may leave a trail.

5

You Gotta Believe

Faith is believing in things when commonsense tells you not to . . . you are going to find out someday that your way of facing this realistic world doesn't work. And when you do, don't overlook those lovely little intangibles. You'll discover that they are the only things that are worthwhile.
—Miracle on 34th Street

We live in a society that is caught up with the maxim "seeing is believing." At times that makes good sense and is the widely-accepted bedrock of modern science. But there is another side of life that is not readily verifiable. It is made up of ethereal notions that cling to the maximum "believing is seeing." Truisms from this angle are readily accepted on faith and hope: I think, therefore I am. There is life after death. An apple a day keeps the doctor away. They are anchored on myths or dreams, life-supporting illusions that are truer than true. Our myths give life meaning and purpose. Without them, we lose our way. Some myths are helpful: Teachers make a difference. Life is governed by a higher power. Others are dysfunctional:

Don't smile until Christmas. War produces peace. Either way, myths are the originators and stewards of our cherished beliefs.

Is God Dead?

A healthy society balances objectivity and interpretation. It subscribes to dynamic interplay or dialogue between facts and symbols, rationality and spirituality. The problem with the present times is that this age-old dynamic tension is out of favor. In 1966, when the cover of *Time* magazine asked, "Is God Dead?," the real message was that myths and symbols no longer served as the underpinning and guideposts of life. This one-sided worldview has prevailed and is evident in business and healthcare. Statistics have replaced leadership intuition in business, and scientific tests have eclipsed clinical judgment in medicine. This is most striking in schools. Teachers' historical beliefs—that they are shaping students' lives or that they are stewards of virtue—have been so battered by standards and standardized tests that their noble calling or purpose receives only a secondary glance. The campaign to bring education in line with the so-called bottom-line convictions of the business world has eroded how much teachers believe in the magic and majesty of what they do. The irony is that most successful businesses have learned to balance the paradoxical connection between profit and purpose. Intangibles—such as people, culture, and noble calling—play a major role in business success.

God Is Alive and Well

Southwest Airline's founder Herb Kelleher passionately conveys to employees the core vow of one of America's most successful airlines:

The freedom that we provide to the American people, the freedom to fly, is really the idealistic and ennobling purpose of

Southwest Airlines and its entire wonderful people. Just as a bricklayer is not just laying bricks, with each brick he lays he is building a home, so too are our people not just answering phones or throwing bags or collecting tickets or maintaining airplanes. We are, each of us as we do these things each day, giving people the freedom to fly; the great service of freedom that you, the people of Southwest Airlines, provide to the people of America is indeed the higher calling and the greater cause that each of us answers each day when we come to work . . . . No other airline brings so much to so many and I thank you for doing that. (Bolman & Deal, 2005, p. 147)

If the people of Starbucks (mentioned in the Introduction) can pour their hearts into a cup coffee and Southwest employees can find an ennobling purpose, higher calling, and greater cause in making air travel available to all people, why can't teachers reclaim the beliefs and rewards in shaping the lives of young people? When Lou Gerstner (also mentioned in the Introduction) became CEO of IBM, he inherited a company that had once been the most admired enterprise in the world but had slumped to one of the most troubled. Originally the hardheaded results-driven manager thought he would steer the company in a radically more goal-oriented direction. He quickly discovered, however, that the company had drifted from its historically anchored values and beliefs. His main job now became one of restoring and revitalizing IBM's soul:

My deepest culture-changing goal was to induce IBMers to believe in themselves again—to believe that they had the ability to determine their own fate, and that they already knew what they needed to know. It was to shake them out of their depressed stupor and remind them of who they were. (Bolman & Deal, 2005, p. 182)

Like IBM, schools have drifted from their core beliefs. It's hard to believe in yourself as a teacher when so many deem you a failure. It's difficult to keep the faith in what you teach when reform pressures constrict the purpose of education to producing results on standardized tests. Top-performing businesses believe that by putting people and purpose first, profits will follow in due course. FedEx's succinct statement of purpose, "People, Service, and Profit . . . in that order," speaks volumes about the company's solemn resolve.

The heartrending problem is that schools and teachers are subjected to the wrong lessons from questionable companies. For some reason, out-of-kilter voices are dominating the policy agenda. Instead of trying to make schools more data and bottom-line driven, we should be encouraging a return to mythical roots to engender their hallowed principles. Doing so would free dedicated teachers to once again believe in themselves and their work, to reclaim their rightful mantle. It would release them to pump some heart, soul, faith, and purpose into a profession too often shackled by pressures that upset the delicate balance between product and passion, mechanics and magic, rationality and spirituality.

THE PYGMALION EFFECT

In medical research, the "placebo effect" is a fact of life. In clinical trials, those who receive the "real" dosage often improve. But just as often positive effects are documented in the control group—those who receive a faux formulation. Scientists explain this observable actuality by concluding that those who get better taking a sugar pill improve because they believe they will. This finding reinforces the traditional maxim, "You have to believe it can happen before it will. If you want to achieve something out of the ordinary, you have to believe you can."

The placebo effect in education was acknowledged some time ago with the fallout of a novel experiment by Rosenthal and Jacobsen (1968). In the fall, they randomly labeled a group of children as "spurters" who were "about to bloom" and could be expected to achieve dramatic growth in the coming school year. And they did. In *Pygmalion in the Classroom*, the experiment's success is attributed to teacher expectations; students succeeded because teachers believed they could. Taking these results at face value shines a new light on the academic failure of minority and low socioeconomic students. They fail because we believe they will and they usually fulfill our expectations.

This may help explain why charter and private schools succeed when public schools fail. It's not the instructional techniques or other technical advantages that make a difference. It is the widely accepted system of beliefs held by teachers and parents and somehow, tangibly or mystically, conveyed to students. The same kind of transformation occurred at the previously mentioned Saturn Corporation when laggard General Motors workers building some of the world's worst automobiles were given another chance. They succeeded because they believed they could, a belief system embedded in the soul of the new manufacturing plant—the Spirit of Saturn. The American public responded by buying into a "different kind of company, a different kind of car." Was the Saturn automobile that special? It really didn't matter because most people believed it was. In the late 1990s, forty-four thousand Saturn owners drove their cars to Spring Hill, Tennessee, to be part of the company's homecoming. The event gave people a chance to see where their cars had been built and an opportunity to thank the workers who built them. The gratitude was mutual as Saturn employees were able to show customers their gratefulness face-to-face "for believing that we could do it."

BELIEF SPAWNS VERVE

If believing is important in the automobile business, it must be next to godliness in education. If you produce a substandard vehicle, it can be reduced to scrap and recycled. If you short-change or damage a student, there is no acceptable recourse. But buttressing a rock-solid belief in the crucial difference that a teacher can make in the lives of students takes more than posting a list of values, articulating a lofty vision, or coming up with an on-paper philosophy that only its authors can decipher. It begins with an exploration of the inner conviction deeply held in the hearts and heads of teaching professionals. No one can really believe in you unless you wholly believe in yourself and your work. Very often teachers lament, like Rodney Dangerfield, that they receive little respect from students, parents, or the community. Rather than complaining about the absence of appreciation, teachers would be better advised to come up with better ways of earning it. To para-phrase Lou Gerstner's message to IBMers, teachers already know what they need to know.

Respect for the teaching profession will follow in due course when teachers regain and display the traditions and beliefs that give them an aura of distinctiveness and render their true work so vital. Giving students the freedom to learn sits above Southwest's offering people the freedom to fly in its importance to society's future. But teachers need to wear the beliefs of their noble undertaking like a badge of honor and a symbol of virtue.

The film *Teachers* depicts a dysfunctional inner-city high school where the principal is out of touch, the teachers have given up, and the students are out of control. Each Monday, many teachers call in sick and finding substitute teachers to cover classes is a chronic problem. Gower, a mental patient from a local institution, mistakenly intercepts a call for Mr. Van Arch from the school secretary who asks if he wants to teach today. He responds in the affirmative and takes over a history class. Substitute teachers are a prime target for the frustrations of students, but before the students can begin their classic harassment, the mental patient collects all the history books and tosses them out the window. The students cheer, thinking they will be freed from learning about events they could care less about. The substitute walks over to the closet and surprises the students by turning around disguised as Abraham Lincoln. He solemnly reads the Declaration of Independence. History has come to life and the students are hooked.

In subsequent days, he adopts the persona of several well-known historical figures. One day, he is General Custer and students enthusiastically question him about his actions that led to the well-known disaster. About that time, the assistant principal discovers that a mental patient is holding forth in one of the school's history classes. Flanked by two white-uniformed attendants from the local mental hospital, he barges into the classroom and orders the attendants to take their wayward patient into custody. The students loudly object because they are learning history for the first time.

By this time, a crowd of students and teachers has assembled along the hallway, "lookey-loos" wanting to see firsthand what the excitement is all about. As the psychiatric attendants are leading their patient through the crowd, he suddenly stops and wrests his arms free. He inquires in a commanding voice, "Don't you know who I am?" An attendant derisively responds, "Yeah. You're General Custer." Drawing himself to full height, throwing his chest outward, and cocking his head defiantly, the patient responds passionately, "I AM A TEACHER, and you shall treat me as such." A hushed sense of reverence falls over the crowd and the attendants soften their grip. Gower has donned the virtuous cloak of a true teacher and invoked the respect that the profession deserves and can demand.

SAVED FROM THE SHARKS

Believing in the revered ideals of education calls forth the mystical potency of education. Its potential influence on students is awesome. Each year students at Vanderbilt University sponsor an event called the Raft Debate as part of the orientation program for entering freshmen. Faculty representing each of the university's schools—Arts and Sciences, Nursing, Medicine, Engineering, Music, and Education—must justify to the cohort of 1,300 entering students why their discipline should be spared while others are thrown to the sharks. The event is one of the highlights of the new school year's beginning, often attended by the provost and chancellor in addition to faculty and staff. The occasion is conducted with ceremonial flair. A mock-up raft occupies the center of the large auditorium's stage. Music from the movie *Jaws* opens the debate. Each faculty member is then given five minutes to present good reason for why his or her profession should be saved from the sharks' jaws. The opening arguments are followed by a rebuttal period. The raft survivor is selected by voice vote of the freshmen.

Historically the education representative had been among the shark bait, never selected to be out of danger on the spacious raft. One year that changed. The education presentation came last in the opening order. The school's representative began,

I'm from the School of Education and wanted to do a fabulous multimedia presentation for you. But teachers don't have much money, so you're going to have to use your imaginations to view my slide show.

With that, the faculty representative pulled from his shirt pocket a twenty-five cent metal clicker popular with children at Halloween. He continued,

First slide. On the screen behind me is a picture of a physician doing surgery. (Click) This is the patient in the morgue following the procedure. (Click) This is the physician on the golf course. (Click) Notice the engineer constructing a bridge. (Click) This is a picture of the bridge taken after it collapsed. (Click) Here is the lawyer arguing the case for his client in front of a jury. (Click) This is his client in a jail cell immediately thereafter.

One by one, the faculty member playfully belittled each profession. Students were riveted by the presentation (afterwards some were sure the slides were in color). Then his jocular, tongue-in-cheek attitude became more reverent. His voice was more reserved but obviously filled with passion:

(Click) Remember her? That's Miss Smith, one your favorite teachers. (Click) Remember him? He was a teacher who believed in you when you doubted yourself. (Click) This is a recent picture of them together. Notice how proud and happy they seem. (Click) This is a group picture of all of you. Now you know why they are smiling. They are proud and happy because they know that there is part of them in each of you, forever. How could you ever throw them to the sharks?

The auditorium exploded in a thunderous roar. All freshmen were on their feet applauding and shouting. The law school professor made a last-ditch effort to salvage the damage. He jumped to the microphone and addressed the now-seated education representative: "Professor, it is said that those who can, do; and those who cannot, teach. Would you like to respond?" The retort was immediate and sharp, "You teach don't you?" Once again, the auditorium erupted in a wild ovation. The debate was over and, for the first time, education was safe and dry on the raft while other schools were fed to the sharks.

PALE GRAY TO HOT PINK

What won the debate was the vivid invocation of the heart and soul of education. The school's representative obviously believed in himself and was passionate about the beliefs undergirding the teaching profession. Those cherished, intangible values are just as powerful now as they were in days past. But in the face of pressures to focus on only what can be standardized and measured, the tradition and magic of teaching has become dormant. The same sort of depressed pale gray stupor described by Gerstner at IBM shrouds too much of the teaching profession today. But gusto and verve can be swiftly revived by courageous people who ardently believe in what they do. The incantation of the ideals of education can be as persuasive for parents and other relevant audiences as it was for the onlookers of the mental patient turned high school teacher or the Vanderbilt University freshmen.

Rekindling the teaching mystique begins with a reflective inner journey to find the original motivating source for a career in education. Entertaining some key questions can help guide the search: Why did I become a teacher? What legacy do I wish to leave to the world? What do I believe in so ardently that I would be willing, like journalists, to go to jail to protect? If no answers come up, then it's time to find other work. If the odyssey rediscovers or reaffirms the hot pink desire to make a difference in shaping young lives, then some tough choices lie ahead.

When top-down demands run counter to the ennobling purpose or higher calling of their profession, teachers have to do some real soul searching and then be prepared to defend their beliefs about the true essence of their work. This will require courage; the will to push ahead even when we are afraid. To paraphrase the Wizard of Oz's message to the Cowardly Lion, "All you need is confidence in yourself."

As mentioned, quality guru W. Edwards Deming maintained that one of the first steps in achieving high-quality outcomes is to "drive fear from the workplace." Teacher Frank McCourt (2005) sums it up in the following:

> I've had to ask myself what the hell I'm doing in the classroom. I've worked out an equation for myself. On the left side of the blackboard print a capital F, on the right side another capital F. I draw an arrow from left to right, from fear to freedom . . . I don't think anyone achieves complete freedom, but what I'm trying to do is drive fear into a corner. (p. 23)

HOT PINK TIGERS

Today, teachers' voices are not being heard by those who make policy that affects life in schools and classrooms. Part of this is caused by fear, some because the classroom is a teacher's private island. But more and more, we are finding out that the school has effects on learning independent of individual classrooms. Policies from above are wending their way into educational practice, upsetting the teeter-totter equilibrium between soul and substance. For teachers, this may be the time to stand behind what they believe to be in the best interests of young people. Teachers very seldom think of themselves as politicians and typically find conflict distasteful. But when standards and testing begin to erode the more intangible influence teachers wield in shaping young lives, unified grassroots political action takes precedent over the comfort of individual autonomy. This is when teachers need to roar. In the political arena, what teachers lack in political clout can be offset by the influence of their expertise and their moral authority:

> *External tools of power have occasional utility in teaching, but they are no substitute for authority, the authority that comes from a teacher's inner life. The clue is in the word itself which has* author *at its core. Authority is granted to people who are perceived as* authoring *their own words, their own actions, their own lives, rather than playing a scripted role at great remove from their own hearts. When teachers depend on the coercive powers of law and technique, they have no authority at all.* (Palmer, 1998, p. 33)

The bottom line for teachers is that the colloquial expression "you gotta believe" has become the order of the decade. Teachers must be willing to stand up for the fundamental truths of education that are threatened by mesmerizing lockstep approaches to learning. Schools don't need more reform;

they need a good dose of revival to reconnect with mystical beliefs about the ennobling of purpose, greater cause, and higher calling within this profession. There are specific steps teachers can take in reviewing, reviving, or reshaping their classrooms and schools. More about that in a later chapter.

6

Setting the Spirit Free

Anomalies are situations that, on the surface, appear to make no sense. You have to look more deeply to find out why. Two researchers set out to investigate anomalies in higher education. They questioned why morale was high in some colleges where conditions were lousy—low salaries, heavy schedules, and run-down facilities. In others, however, morale was low although comparable conditions were extremely favorable. What was the distinguishing factor? Colleges with poor circumstances and high morale had a robust spirit, intangible but discernable to anyone walking onto the campus. The spiritual halo was rooted in history and nourished in countless symbolic ways. As the researchers noted, "A palpable feeling was in the air. You couldn't see or touch it. But you could feel it" (personal communication with Professor Anne Austin).

Spirit plays a similar role in organizations across the board. Ritz-Carlton hotels and Nordstrom department stores, for example, have very high standards. Both also have an uncommon spirit that infuses work with meaning and sets them apart from competitors in their respective business sectors. This tends to be true of most high-performing organizations.

High standards without the vital essence of spirit to rally people create an autocratic system of fear and mechanical conformity. High spirit, on the other hand, can get people revved up. But without specific touchstones to shoot for, employees often fritter away energy on things that don't really matter. Recall the collapse of Enron or WorldCom. Standards and spirit must be in harmony for an enterprise to succeed over the long haul.

We have known for an extended period that the culture of an organization shapes people's behavior and performance. Schools are no exception. Culture can either enhance spirit or dampen the enthusiasm and vitality we all long for at work. A positive, cohesive, and zestful school draws teachers and students together in a common quest, yielding bountiful dividends. The problem is that the aims of educational reforms either ignore or set out to change historically anchored traditional ways. Federal or state reformers strive to remold schools as more rational, technical, and goal-driven places. And school administrators very often emphasize similar logical expectations. It's what they learn in their formal training and how they see their roles.

Inattention coupled with overly technical remedies has caused the ancestral way of life in many schools to wither, creating barren places for the age-old act of teaching and learning. Teaching becomes just a job and teachers go through the motions with little joy or commitment. A teacher lamented recently:

> *Sometimes I think my job today could be handled by someone supervising students working on computerized, instructional programs. Her task would be maintaining order and keeping students on task. Motivation would be built into the linear programs. An outside firm could be retained to handle the testing. That's not why I became a teacher.*

Over time, without attention, the spiritual side of schools gives way to sterility and toxicity. Both teachers and students have to function in a bleak or festering environment where negativity is the common thread and fear, mistrust, and intrigue prevail. It doesn't have to be that way.

Lou Gerstner (2002), the executive mentioned earlier, commented on the crucial role of culture in business success. "I came to see in my time at IBM that culture isn't just one aspect of the game—it is the game" (p. 182). Gerstner soon learned that revival, not a complete overhaul, was the most promising way to go. Gerstner's role became one of pulling forward and breathing new life into old, still viable cultural forms and practices. What he learned in the business world is equally applicable to schools and classrooms. Today's teachers and administrators need to seize the torch from a blanket move toward uniform standards and uniform testing. They can counterbalance its technical accent with the spiritual emphasis of culture and tradition. It can be accomplished by giving history, values, heroes, ritual, ceremony, and stories a more prominent place on the educational agenda. The primary mission is to breathe heart, soul, and spirit into classrooms and schools.

THE LEGACY OF HISTORY

As emphasized in previous chapters, the past shapes the present. *History* offers a treasure trove of lessons of what to do and what to avoid in today's situations. Without a sense of where we've come from, we end up making the same mistakes again and again. Reconnecting with our roots from time to time accentuates our identity and renews common bonds with others. Too many organizations are ahistorical. Their amnesia often spawns a drift, like Starbucks, from original values and beliefs that launched an enormously successful enterprise. Revisiting history is one way to revive the collective spirit.

Under the leadership of Jane Kowal, the West Palm Beach School District administrators took a journey together down memory lane. People were asked to form groups around the era they joined the system and then review the highlights of their decade. They were then invited to present the essence of their reminisces to the entire group. People initially balked at the assignment, but quickly plunged into the task. The room filled with energy. The sixties decade walked out, highlighting the disruptive teacher walkout of that period.

Following lunch, each group presented the key events of its period through skits, songs, and poems. The room crackled with electricity and laughter as the amateur pageant unfolded. A newspaper reporter, one of the district's most vocal critics, was drawn into the production. The next day he wrote one of his first positive articles about the district's schools.

Another system kicked off the new school year by inviting students from the past to share their recollections with the assembled teachers and staff. The first surprise came when many of the teachers' biggest problems had become noteworthy successes. But the real payoff came when the former students thanked teachers for the vital influence on their lives. Staff members were also singled out for recognition. An older bus driver was credited for going beyond his official duties to get students to school and back home with a good attitude. Very often he quizzed them on homework assignments. The opening day ended with students giving their former mentors an extended round of applause.

An elementary principal gave the school's seasoned veterans a prominent spot in the orientation of newcomers. The old-timers reconstructed the school's history, letting new teachers know how the culture had evolved over time. Later that week, the principal said that the event had made a marked difference in the attitudes of new teachers, but had an even more powerful impact on the veterans. She concluded, "The only thing worse than not hearing the history was knowing the past and having no one to listen."

Having a sense of history is a necessary part of creating a cohesive culture focused on the development of young lives. This key point is overlooked by reform initiatives that consider the past either irrelevant or a barrier to improvement.

THE POTENCY OF SYMBOLS AND SLOGANS

History spawns and perpetuates *core values and beliefs*. It documents and dramatizes how these crucial cornerstones of spirit emerged. To be effective, values and beliefs require summary symbols that express and make accessible more complex guiding principles. These are more than advertising slogans. They are brands that keep an organization's vows uppermost in people's minds and hearts. Shorthand symbols also convey an organization's image to outsiders. Symbolically the slogan "every child a promise" communicates what a school system stands for. Often, values and beliefs are conveyed through tangible images. The red and white circular target of Target stores says a lot about the corporation. It is used in all its commercials, very often to the exclusion of specifics. The apple is a universal symbol of teaching and expresses meaning well beyond its literal status as a fruit. So does the Nike swoosh. A formal statement of vision, values, or beliefs communicates very little unless distilled into an accessible form that is memorable, emotional, and meaningful.

A Colorado school district convened an all-day educational summit. The event drew representatives from across community organizations: police and fire chiefs, the mayor, city officials, business people, homemakers, physicians and other healthcare professionals, city workers, teachers, and students. The topic for discussion was the purpose of education. After a large meeting of the entire assembly, heterogeneous groups mixing the various interests had lunch together in local restaurants. After lunch, the groups reconvened to delve into a highly difficult undertaking—identifying the essence of teaching and learning. Their deliberations were facilitated by local high school students. When the groups returned to the large assembly, each group presented the results of its discussions. Interestingly, there was consensus across groups about the purposes of education, heavily weighted toward character development, civic responsibility, working with others, and both critical and creative thinking.

As the summit came to a close, a key question was posed: Where do test scores fit into the picture? Educators were charged with the responsibility of developing better indicators for assessing district progress toward fulfilling the community's shared expectations for its schools. Standardized scores, measuring basic skills, were an important part of the mix. But the community wanted the average yearly progress of schools to include a broader spectrum of outcomes. The district now had a common charter. In addition to reaching an agreement on educational principles, the summit created a renewed community spirit in support of its public schools.

THE INSPIRATION OF HEROES

Slogans, symbols, and emblems are important in capturing elusive values. *Heroes* play a supplementary role. Heroes are living icons whose words and deeds are emblematic of a desired moral code. Even deceased heroes live on, still playing a role expressing the symbolic vows of a community. Heroes are looked up to for the desirable ideals they represent. Students very often cast their teachers as heroic figures. Teachers model attributes students wish to emulate—"When I grow up, I want to be just like him." They spot talent before students see it themselves—"She saw I had talent—before I saw it myself. She told me I had something special—and that made all the difference." They encourage students to chart a worthy course, whatever the risks—"Listen to your heart, and once it defines a path, take it. The worst that can happen is you fail. Then you try again."

When we celebrate heroes we put cultural values on display. When we ignore them we lose a promising chance to summon the collective spirit and risk losing our inimitable icons. Following a major effort to change the district's system of evaluating teachers, a classroom teacher was responding to queries about the reform's impact. The interview session was pro forma up to a point. Suddenly, the interviewer scanned the classroom from his vantage point, sitting uncomfortably in a small elementary classroom chair. The room was very familiar as it reminded him of his stint in second grade. He became very excited, asking the teacher if she still taught students about the music staff and the bass and treble clef. She got up, went to the blackboard and used the five-pronged instrument to form the music staff's five lines. She then taught an impromptu lesson just like the ones he remembered. She never missed a beat. Excitedly he said, "That's magic. It must be so rewarding to be a teacher." She erupted with stories about her experiences with students over the years. As she wound down, he asked why she hadn't shared that richness before. She responded, "Why should you care? No one around here does anymore." He again asked her opinion about the new approach to evaluating teachers. "Oh, I just go along with that because I'm a good sport. It doesn't have anything to do with my teaching." The district missed a bet in not celebrating that teacher and others like her. A celebration of heroes would probably do far more good than revising the approach to teacher evaluation.

One enduring virtue of heroic figures is the sanctification of their rightful license to anoint other heroes. Such public recognition goes a long way in communicating what an organization stands for, its spiritual commitments. An Oregon elementary school has as its watchwords "Always Reach For Excellence." This is meant to encourage teachers and students to go for it, reaching far above the ground to do their best. The principal has created a wall in a hallway to honor the heroic accomplishments of students. When someone reaches well beyond their scholastic limits, the principal summons the entire school community—including parents—into the hallway. There she paints the student's hand with paint, has him or her slap the wall with a "high five" and then writes the student's name beside the handprint along with the accomplishment. The school's Hall of Honor is living testimony to the laudable exploits of students and encourages others to join the wall's pantheon.

Creating heroes goes on at all levels of education, often spontaneous and unplanned. A university professor was trying to encourage a class of 200 undergraduates to think for themselves. He wasn't making much headway as students persisted in accepting without question everything he said. During a lecture he wanted to see how bizarre he could get before students took him to task. He told them the world was actually flat. Students wrote it down. He then corrected himself maintaining the earth was actually oblong, suspended to the moon. Erasers made way for a new revelation. He kept on and, heads down, students' pencils flipped from point to end. Finally, a young female raised her hand. He recognized her and she confidently observed, "Professor, I think you're full of shit." An eerie silence gripped the classroom. Except for one student all eyes were riveted on notebooks. The professor asked her for her reasoning behind the statement. Without hesitation she listed her reasons. He responded, "Felicia, following your criteria, you are absolutely right and I am shocked that no one else had the courage to make an argument public before now. Thank you."

Later, the student came to see the professor. "You'll never know how much that meant to me. I've always been put down for speaking my mind. You made me a champion in the eyes of other students. You reinforced who I really am." The student is now the vice president of a large hotel chain. She calls periodically to tell the professor that when she has an unpopular opinion, she remembers the class and then forcefully makes her point. She credits her forthrightness as part of her rapid rise through managerial ranks.

THE BONDING OF RITUALS

Rituals are meaningful actions that we do over and over again. They are different from habits which are done repeatedly without a real instrumental payoff. Rituals are connected to those things that are difficult to express in language. They contain spiritual codes that bond people with core values and beliefs and to each other. They are enacted in the same sequence each time. Straying from the traditional order would undercut their mystical power. To return to Professor Myers of a previous chapter, any changes in his classroom sequence of bursting through the door, slamming his briefcase on the lectern, and flinging open the same window would have been disturbing. It would somehow have diluted the special influence his courses had on the hearts of students.

People everywhere have their special cultural rites. It is just as true in the workplace as it is in the surrounding culture. All professions observe their distinctive ways. What appears to be a superficial set of actions to outsiders knits insiders together and puts them in an apt frame of mind to do their work successfully. Physicians scrub for seven minutes before doing a surgical procedure. While the necessity of the prolonged scrub is open to question with the advent of modern germicides, its traditional role in preparing the surgical team for a delicate procedure is unassailable. In the airline business, the first officer deplanes the aircraft and conducts a walk-around inspection before takeoff. Very seldom do they discover something amiss. But symbolically it prepares the cockpit crew for their awesome responsibility of getting all the souls aboard safely to their destinations.

Rituals in schools take many different forms. Some are simple, while others are more elaborate. But it's always the below-the-surface subtext that conveys the symbolic message. Most students reassemble after the noon recess with little joy. Raging adrenaline and sedentary classroom routine don't mix well. Mrs. Krantz, an experienced fifth-grade teacher in a small rural school had come up with a way to smooth the transition with a pedagogical payoff. Her third-grade students look forward to the end of the lunch period. They know that while they catch their breath and rest their heads on their desks she will begin the afternoon by reading another chapter of Nancy Drew or the Hardy Boys. Her reading plays an important transition role. But symbolically it reinforces how reading can transport people to different places, kindling their imaginations and encouraging them to read more on their own. Students learn to read when they themselves discover the liberating spirit of the written word.

As another example, students in Mrs. Harris's third-grade class knew precisely how their school day would begin. It was her twist on an opening ritual, done the same way, every day.

Mrs. Harris, my third-grade teacher, was quite a sharp dresser. She wore beautiful high heels. Sometimes she switched to flats in the afternoon if her feet got tired, but every morning began with the click, click, click of her high heels as she greeted us up and down the rows. (Ladson-Billings, 1994, p. 36)

Don't be underwhelmed at the simplicity of these two examples. Ritual is not judged by its literal sequence. Its influences are determined by what it means. In some classrooms, rituals are more elaborate. Mrs. Harris teaches in a chaotic multiracial school. But her classroom is like a calm place in the midst of a raging storm. Ritual is one reason why.

Mrs. Harris starts her second-grade class each morning with a song. One of her children's favorites is "Peace Is Flowing Like a River." She begins instruction by asking, "What are we going to be our best at today?" Students start volunteering ideas, both instructional and noninstructional, at which they intend to excel. "I'm going to be good at my math," says one little boy. "I'm gonna be good at lining up for recess," shouts another. "I'm gonna be good at doing my own work and minding my own business," says a little girl. As the students recite their goals and expectations for the day, Mrs. Harris encourages them with a smile or a comment—"Oh, you are? Well, that's very good!" or "I just know you can do that."

At the end of the day, Harris reconvenes her students to have them assess how well they met their goals. Each student is given an opportunity to describe what she or he did to be successful during the day. Students report on successes and reflect on ways they could have been even better at some things. Harris constantly tells them how good they are. (Ladson-Billings, 1994, p. 48)

Schoolwide rituals knit teachers, students, and administrators together in a common quest for learning. In a Texas elementary school, each day begins with an assembly replete with a school song, the Pledge of Allegiance, and a collective commitment to today's learning objectives. A middle school in Connecticut sets aside a half hour each day where everyone in the school—teachers, students, administration, and staff—stops what they are doing and reads. In an interesting twist, the principal noticed that the school custodian was reading his book upside down. Further probing found that the custodian was illiterate. Teachers volunteered to give the custodian lessons in learning to read. He now serves as a living testimony to the school's emphasis on reading.

Ritual unites people together and its subtext symbolically reinforces common ties which words cannot express. In today's multicultural world, schools include students of many dialects. Beneath each dialect is a patchwork of unique cultural traditions. Ritual helps build a common bridge among students with different cultural backgrounds. This helps to cultivate a hearty spirit that unifies students under a jointly owned cultural canopy.

THE GRANDEUR OF CEREMONIES

Periodic *ceremonies* put cultural values and accomplishments on public display to be celebrated and appreciated. Top-performing corporations are renowned for elaborate ceremonies. Mary Kay Cosmetic's annual seminars feature pink Cadillacs, diamond bumblebee pins, and the crowning of its top beauty consultants. The bumblebee, which aerodynamically is incapable of flight, represents the "can-do" spirit that motivates people to move beyond what appears impossible. The event summons the company's unique character and revs people up for the year ahead. The soul of the company becomes manifest in the festivities.

Schools also have celebrations. Colleges and universities begin the year with a convocation and end with a commencement. In Concord, Massachusetts, the high school was having problems. Parents got together and hosted an evening celebration of teachers. There was a piano bar with wine and cheese, the cafeteria had been gussied up with white tablecloths and candelabras. Upon arrival, teachers were given a boutonniere or corsage with the various synonyms for teacher—guru, mentor, guide, and coach. Parents and teachers gathered around the piano bar and sang familiar old tunes. After a resplendent dinner the student choir sang songs related to teaching. Then the entire crowd rose to their feet to give teachers a standing ovation. The superintendent reported shortly after that the event changed the valence of the school from negative to positive in a miraculous way.

Too often reforms either give celebrations low priority or squelch them altogether. For example, in a Southern California elementary school, students of the month are recognized in a public ceremony. Parents, teachers, and other students are present. Over the year, students are singled out for special recognition highlighting the various talents the school values most. At the end of each year, all students receive some form of recognition. At the occasion, honorees are called in front of the audience and the principal reads words of commendation written by the teachers. Recently the administration decided that reading the students' accomplishments took too long. If the parents had enough time they were asked back to the classroom to hear the teacher's comments. They were not read publicly in the main event. As a result the celebration lost much of its zest and oomph and people were disappointed. Cutting ceremonial occasions short dampens the spirit. Too often today's schools overlook the value of setting aside time for special occasions.

Celebrations should always commemorate beginnings and endings. In a Pennsylvania school district, the superintendent began each school year by lighting the "lamp of learning" with all his teachers and staff in attendance. In Tucson, Arizona, the superintendent convened all 5,000 employees at the kickoff of the new school year. Student musical groups representing all of the district's multicultural traditions reminded people of the district's diverse clientele. An outside speaker gives a motivational talk about the importance of the entire school community in educating young people.

Some schools celebrate the end of the school year. At a Chicago elementary school, teachers did a rendition of the farewell song from *The Sound of Music.* Melodies and lyrics have a way of surfacing sentiments and memories that normal discourse cannot get in touch with. The mood of the students was sad, but also full of glee. The melodic interlude helped both the students and the teachers mark the transition of school days to summer vacation.

In any school there are hundreds of things to celebrate if people are willing to take the time and give special events a central place. Ceremonies summon the spirit of the school and unify people toward a common vista. Many attribute such events to elevated educational performance.

THE MAGIC OF STORIES

It has been said that God created people because he loves *stories.* Stories carry values, extol the virtues of heroes, and serve as fodder for elegant ceremonies. It is no secret to members of Congress that a significant amount of legislation is passed with the support of a few dramatic stories. Information provides the backdrop, but good stories carry the day.

Schools are chock-full of first-rate stories. Some of the narratives are humorous because schools are filled with students whose adventures or misadventures warm the heart. The administration of a middle school was faced with a persistent problem. Young girls were constantly putting on lipstick and kissing the mirror in the girls' bathroom. It was a form of tagging, but a pain in the neck to clean up. All attempts to correct the situation failed. Then the custodian said to the administrators, "I think I can fix this problem." He invited some of the well-known culprits into the girls' bathroom. He explained to them how difficult it was for him to keep cleaning the mirror several times during the school day. He told them he wanted to show them how difficult it was. He took a rag, walked over to toilet, wet the rag, and proceeded to wipe off the mirror. That simple remedy worked. The word got around, and no lipstick appeared on the mirror again.

Many of the stories in schools are inspirational. For example, an older teacher pulled a keynote speaker aside and asked if he'd like to hear another good story. He pointed to the watch on his wrist, and asked the presenter if he could tell what made it so special. The obvious answer was that it was an $8,000 Rolex watch, but the real story was the circumstance where the teacher received the watch. As the teacher recounted the event, years ago he had an at-risk student in class whose mother was a prostitute and father was a convicted drug dealer. The teacher had looked behind the surface disadvantages. He saw something special in the student. He did whatever he could to support him and show him that he believed in his potential. The student went on to become one of the most successful businessmen in the local community. After many years had passed he was at the teacher's door with a wrapped package. When Mr. Jones opened the gift he was taken aback. It contained a gold Rolex watch. The former student said, "Mr. Jones, I want you to have this watch." The teacher explained that he could not accept such an expensive gift. The student then said, "Mr. Jones, I want you to have this watch. Everyone but you in my life thought I was a piece of s---. You were the only one who believed in me. And, besides, you must accept the watch because I have inscribed it to you." The teacher looked at the back of the watch, and it was inscribed, "To Mr. Jones, Love, Johnny." As he ended the story, the teacher disappeared into the crowd.

At the end of his presentation the speaker invited Mr. Jones to come forward and tell the story to the large assembly of teachers. He did and every teacher in the crowd suddenly came to realize what a difference one can teacher can make in the life of another human being.

Those stories convey the true spirit of teaching which, too often, is subordinate to the mechanics of the profession. It's hard to imagine either humorous or inspirational stories emerging from test preparation and the nose-to-the-grindstone standards that guide schools today. It is sad to think that many modern businesses are more soulful than today's schools. Neglecting the time-honored cultural traditions in education undercuts the intended purpose of school reform legislation. Time spent focusing on history, values, heroes, rituals, ceremonies, and stories is one of the chief ways to summon the true élan of schools. In doing so, we may achieve many of the intended goals of No Child Left Behind and other reform efforts. By relying more on spiritual and cultural traditions rather than rational and technical strategies, we may help shape schools everyone can be proud of. Now is the time to put culture on the front rather than the back burner.

7

Speaking Up

Voices From the Trenches

In 2008, No Child Left Behind comes up for reauthorization. As we write, the battle lines are being drawn. Representative George Miller (D-Calif.), Chair of the House education committee, has proposed an expansion of measures used to track student progress. He will introduce growth models that look at the achievement of individual students rather than aggregated test scores of cohorts. Other measures under consideration include student portfolios, formative assessments, and graduation rates. Otherwise, Miller predicts there are not enough votes to support reauthorization.

The Republican members of the committee, on the other hand, appear to disfavor loosening the law to permit multiple measures. A staff member of the Republicans stated their position, "We are very uncomfortable with things that are hard to measure being lumped in with the accountability system. Any thing that is not directly tied to student achievement is a problem for us" (Gill, 2007, p. 25).

The coming battle for reauthorization centers on the tangible results controversy. Many legislators and analysts believe that, unless something can be measured, it lacks validity and reliability. Others maintain that, if you probe below the rational veneer of test scores and political rhetoric, a different story emerges. This account portrays some elusive consequences that threaten the very core of NCLB's purported purposes. Like a new drug, the program's unintended side effects may be far worse than the anticipated cure. Often, these unforeseen costs are intangible and difficult to link to their bona fide source. Even so, the effects, like rising dropout rates or disaffected teachers, are real.

Especially disturbing in the current debate is the recurrently overlooked erosion of the magical side of teaching. To many educators teaching is a calling; a solemn commitment to making a real difference in a young person's life. It's not tangible. It's not easily measured, but it's very genuine. In our exploration of NCLB's impact we have looked closely at an aspect of teaching that is, unfortunately, relegated to second place if it qualifies at all. But herein lies the paradox. Example after example of parents, teachers, and students chronicling the indelible imprint of good teaching warms the heart and enlivens the soul.

TUNING OUT, SIGNING UP, OR SPEAKING OUT?

Hirschman (1970), in his influential book *Exit, Voice and Loyalty,* concluded that people in organizations have a finite number of choices in dealing with changing circumstances. They can sign up and become loyal followers of a new regime or regimen. They can exit by either tuning out or shipping out. Or they can use their voices to speak up and challenge changes that don't make much sense. Each option bears both benefits and risks. When each person in an organization signs up, it creates potential for an ensemble—a unified group of individuals working as one to accomplish a shared mission. The problem is that very few teachers are signing on to the standardization and narrow accountability of NCLB. Many conform because they see no options. They go through the motions with little heart or commitment, squirreling away time to do what makes school exciting and meaningful. Their struggle is having to play the game dictated from above rather than doing what they believe is in the best interests of young people. This creates cognitive and emotional dissonance.

Some choose to exit. They either are dropping out physically, leaving the profession for more meaningful work, or disengaging on the job—mentally and spiritually. The drawbacks of this strategy are both personal and societal. Personally, the demands of seeking a new career and leaving one's calling for other work can be harsh. Society loses because the teachers who are leaving may be some of the most talented and creative "veteran teachers and more dynamic, creative young teachers are more likely than ever to leave the profession, disgusted by the tedium of drill-and-kill and saddened by the lack of time or freedom to engage their students in the excitement of learning interesting stuff" (Gill, 2007, p. 35).

Very few teachers are speaking up, registering publicly and forcefully their opposition or advocating assertively for a better way to educate young people. They did not enter the profession to become politicians or lobbyists. Most are neither willing nor equipped to enter the policymaking arena. They enjoy the direct face-to-face experience of teaching rather than indirectly and remotely influencing the goings-on at national and state capitols. Unfortunately, when teachers do speak up, their voices do not seem to catch the ears of policymakers who make the rules. If they did, things would be very different.

TEACHERS SPEAK THEIR MINDS

Collectively, the voices of teachers can be unusually powerful. They are in direct contact with students every day. They know firsthand what works and what doesn't. We offered a random sample of teachers an opportunity to tell how NCLB and other reforms look from their point of view. Here are some examples of what teachers would say to legislators if given the opportunity to be heard.

A high school math teacher responds:

No Child Left Behind (NCLB) is another sounds-good idea that has been poorly implemented. It would be hard to find someone who would disagree with the notion that teachers should teach. Very few teachers strongly oppose being monitored to gauge if they are teaching their students, but NCLB goes beyond what they are comfortable with.

NCLB is designed to have all students reach a designated point at a certain time. Not all students are capable of reaching all points at the same time. As an example, let's look at middle school math. NCLB suggests that all eighth-grade students should be proficient in algebra by the time they enter high school. One wonders if this is a reasonable expectation. High school math teachers are saying that more students are entering high school burnt out by algebra than ever before. Forcing students to take algebra too soon dooms them to failure. They get the feeling that they are incapable of doing algebra, when in actuality they only failed because they were forced to take the class before they were properly prepared to do so. It is undeniable the some eighth-grade students, maybe even most eighth-grade students, can take algebra and succeed just fine. On the other hand, it is simply unreasonable to expect all of them to.

NCLB was implemented to force schools to improve the education they were offering to lower achieving students. Parts of its implementation are actually harming the same students it was designed to help. Some students need more time than others to succeed in some areas. Give them that time. It is all right to measure achievement or growth. It is counterproductive to expect all students to reach a plateau at the same time. Let's keep students progressing at a reasonable rate. Some will progress faster than we may expect, but others may take a little more time. NCLB offers little patience thereby dashing hopes of potential payoff.

Many teachers are working in school districts with high percentages of underrepresented students. A Latino educator responds with the following:

> *While the overall picture of NCLB's intent is clear, there are still many questions I have of how our school districts and schools should interpret what No Child Left Behind truly means. Working in a predominately Hispanic district, I can understand how the intended fairness of NCLB could be for minority students, but I just don't see this happening. Just how are we to ensure that every child receives a fair and just education? For openers there should be a parent version of NCLB so they can understand their role in their child's education. I, for one, would love to see a workable program that would ensure every child in our country receive a chance to succeed.*

A middle school history teacher writes:

> *The No Child Left Behind Act (NCLB), on paper, is reputed by some a national success. Across the country school districts point to an alleged rise in test scores in both English and math. However, sometimes looks can be deceiving. When one establishes parameters to be met, intelligent individuals inevitably will find ways to achieve the documented success necessary, while students will be shortchanged in the classroom. For instance, seventh-grade students are educated in the field of algebraic basics and even parts of the periodic table. Yet, ask them the capital of the United States, or what county they live in, and they are clueless.*
>
> *These problems will persist as long as we live in a society where test scores hurt schools, administrators, teachers, and benefit politicians. It is politicians that set the standards the American youth must live up to, not educators. And, since most politicians are not educators, they simply have no grasp of what this program's lingering effect on education will be. Already, teachers and administrators are not walking, but running*

toward the exits in droves. They simply have had enough. Teachers no longer want to spend their own time meeting with consultants with no classroom experience. Administrators are cracking under the pressure of the policy in a no-win situation. The idea of putting teachers through rigorous qualification testing is driving potential educators from the profession. All the while, politicians, with no experience, sit back and point a smug finger at educators, telling voters who is to blame and how they will personally fix the problem. This is how elections are won, not how problems are solved.

A soon-to-be teacher expresses her views in the following:

I am a concerned prospective teacher. I have not had the opportunity to work full time in a school and experience the impact that NCLB is having on staff members as well as students. What I've observed in schools makes me nervous about my career in teaching. I agree with parts of the foundation of NCLB. I agree that our schools need to be accountable and that our schools need good, quality teachers. However, I do feel there are some parts that are not realistic. In assessing the students' learning, teachers look at "all" students within a grade level as being equal regardless of special accommodations. It is my understanding that all students are assessed within their grade level in state testing, whether limited English proficient or special needs. I don't think this is fair to our schools or our students when they are treated as the norm. I also look at the 2014 date set for all students to read and do math at grade level. I think about the students and teachers who are being affected by NCLB and think, where they will be seven years from now. Where will they be if the program doesn't work? President Bush will no longer be in office so who will be held accountable if NCLB doesn't measure up?

I am not opposed to taking a job in a program improvement school; however, I have to admit I am nervous. I think about the stress that is put on teachers to raise test scores, which leads to teaching to the test. What about the stress put on the students to do well on these tests? We are preparing our students to be test-taking machines. Many of our schools have had to cut out programs and extracurricular activities. There is less time to focus on other core subjects such as social science or physical education in their everyday curriculum. The curriculum focuses almost exclusively on reading, writing, and math. The time that is allotted for "content time" is approximately twenty minutes. This is twenty minutes to teach in any of the following areas: art, science, social science, and physical education. How realistic is it to expect a teacher to teach a lesson and have the students practice the lesson in that time frame? I know that many schools have cut extracurricular activities to focus on the core subjects.

Going into the field of teaching is new for me, and I would like it to remain in my career until I retire. I fear the stress that NCLB puts on schools, teachers, and students may force me to look into another field. I will not know this outcome until I begin teaching permanently; however, I do realize it could be a possibility.

A high school math teacher expresses concerns:

The intent behind the No Child Left Behind legislation was both honorable and needed. With the legislation coming up for renewal I would like to discuss some changes needed. I would agree with the idea of accountability for the education of our nation's youth. Everyone must be accountable for their part in this process. Teachers must have standards that they are required to teach. Administrators need to assure that each student placed in a teacher's classroom has the prerequisite skills needed to learn the new material. Students must be held accountable for doing their best. Many times students do not perform with their maximum effort in school. Parents must be held accountable for their part in their children's education. They must make sure that their child is at school on time and receives at least eight hours of sleep each night. They need to make sure their child completes each homework assignment on time. Legislators must be held accountable for their actions. Education must be properly funded to meet the needs of students. If legislation such as NCLB is passed, it must be properly funded.

There must be consequences for each group of people when they do not perform their responsibilities. When teachers choose not to teach the required material, they should be removed from the classroom. When administrators overcrowd classrooms or do not provide the needed resources to teachers, they should be relieved of their duties. When students do not try in the classroom and at home, they should be removed from the regular education setting and placed in another program. When parents do not require their children to do their homework, get enough sleep, and to be at school, they should lose the right to parent. When legislators do not provide a fair and equitable system that provides the required funding for education, they should be drummed out of office, not waiting for the next election, but removed immediately.

All these eloquent letters laud NCLB's noble intentions. But unanimously they underscore the limitations and failings when its desired aims are put into practice. Who knows better how things really work than those intimately engaged with students day to day? What teachers express verbally here relates mainly to the more technical aspect of instruction, the tangible lessons. But if you probe behind their technical concerns, there lurks a deeper, less conscious realization that the real bliss of being a teacher is in jeopardy. Schools provide students with opportunities to develop in many ways, not just academically.

BALANCING METRICS AND MAGIC

It's a play within a play. What is highlighted onstage is not as crucial as what typically transpires behind the scenes. Teachers play a powerful role in making a difference in how the next generation will turn out. This is not easy to put a figure on. It is exceedingly difficult to articulate especially to those with a hard-nosed, narrow conception of what schools are really about. But the softer side of teaching it is at the very core of why schools exist and what they can do for young people. Achieving a balance between measurement and magic would go a long way in improving the quality of American education. But, this will require a lot more attention to the spiritual underbelly of teaching and learning. Expanding and unifying the voices to be heard in renewing NCLB or considering alternative reform efforts will go a long way to achieving the balance between precision and passion that is sorely needed.

This worthy mission will not come to fruition through independent "voices in the wilderness" nor through individual letters directed at key decision makers. Every change is political and unless your interests have a "place at the table," where bargains are struck, deals made, and legislation passed, you miss the boat. Every major change in this century has come from concerted political action: voting rights for women, civil rights legislation, and better working conditions for migrant farm workers. Most recently, a massive walkout of workers, students, and other supporters hammered home the crucial contribution of undocumented workers to our economy. In education, the interests of special needs students are well represented by an influential joining together of parents, lobbyists, and legislators. For teachers generally, the militancy of the American Federation of Teachers (AFT) and later the National Education Association (NEA) significantly improved their salaries and working conditions. Now the teacher unions could do with widening their focus and advocating just as aggressively on behalf of the existential underpinnings of the profession. Political clout of educators needs to be ratcheted up to get a vital point across; we cannot sacrifice the life-enhancing, long-term influences of teachers to quick-fix accountability.

What we need is a battle-ready coalition of teachers, parents, students, and other groups with similar interests to march on Washington, D.C. or their state capitols. Civil rights legislation in this country to correct a long-standing blunder depriving a group of people their God-given rights happened through aggressive and persistent political action. It was capped off by Martin Luther King's legendary speech. His was a collective dream "deeply rooted in the American dream." He pulled forward and embellished the values on which our country was founded. All Americans are created equal. Political clout was fortified with symbolic virtue. In the same way, we have to march and fight for the traditional and hallowed purposes of education and the vital role teachers play in that noble pursuit

To repair and reshape NCLB, we need a powerful one-two punch. First, we need a vocal coalition of those who feel the consequences of the legislation firsthand: students, teachers, and parents. This alliance might also attract some legislators who could get beyond the prevailing group-think approach to school reform and remember back to caring teachers who helped them along. Banding together those who are not afraid to speak up, who are willing to register forcefully their concerns and suggestions may beget a less industrial and punitive, more organic and people-centered approach to teaching and learning. Of course this tack will produce opposition from many quarters, including parents who are more invested in how their kids stack up and can compete than their passion for learning and personal growth. But the opposing forces can be countered by a simple historical fact. We have been playing the same reform game for far too long with a paltry win-loss record. Now may be the time to seize upon a new and more effective strategy.

Next, we need a rallying symbol or emblem. How about the apple? It has some deep historical roots. In sixteenth century Scandinavia, teachers were very poorly paid. To supplement their meager earnings students brought them baskets of apples, a common crop in ample supply. As wages improved the gift was pared to a single apple, a custom that has survived in a symbolic way to the present. The apple fits the bill as an image or icon that, recalling *Built To Stick*, is relatively unexpected, concrete, credible, emotional, and tells a story. Creating such a slogan or banner for good teaching should come easy, as it was for the education professor who won the Vanderbilt University Raft Debate. Two imaginary teachers from the past provoked students' memories and captured the moment against the persuasion of other professions.

The symbolic high road can also be championed by Susan B. Anthony (Suffragette Movement), César Chávez (Farm Workers), or Martin Luther King-like, magnetic spokespeople or heroes who can sway and unite the troops around a passionate, poetic vision. In education, that image would capitalize on nourishing the individual interests and talents of all students. Teachers would become guides to support students' unique growth from within rather than imposing a predetermined mold from an external source. Schools would radiate heart and soul and become treasured havens in their local communities.

Is this a Pollyannaish, unreachable aspiration? Think back to the civil rights movement. It took a committed coalition of people to stand up for what they believed and lay claim to rights and privileges that were rightfully theirs. They chose to speak up and take risks so that their voices could be heard and remedy an untenable situation. Now is the time for educators to follow their example and breathe some soul into school reform and pump some heart and spirit into teaching.

8

Charting a New Course

Throughout the book we have harped on one especially poignant point: The relentless erosion of the magical side of teaching that has shifted education in a disturbing direction. To many educators teaching is a calling, a solemn commitment to making a real difference in a young person's life. It's mystical and hard to apprehend. Unfortunately, magic is frequently relegated second to measurement if it qualifies at all. Stripping education of its traditional pillars has its price in, among other things, demoralized teachers, disengaged students, and meaningless work. Teachers feel the bind of having to do things they suspect won't work, all the while knowing from experience what does. Students lose sight of what an education offers and vote with their feet. Parents search urgently for some signs that their faith in schools and teachers is justified.

HIDDEN COSTS

There are some even higher, long-term social costs to bear if we stay on the regimented course that top-down reforms have plotted. The consequences go well beyond the immediate losses of demoralized teachers, concerned parents, and more dropouts. The future may mortgage or default on the perpetuation of our free and entrepreneurial way of life. Such a prophecy may seem overly pessimistic. But let's consider the possibilities of such a dire forecast and entertain some promising new tacks to achieve a more hopeful outcome.

Today's students are tomorrow's leaders. They will become teachers, craftspeople, soldiers, lawyers, factory workers, administrators, business owners, physicians or nurses, and legislators. What they are learning now will shape the way they carry out their respective duties later and will govern the kind of people they eventually become. We need to examine today's schools in the light of what the future may demand from educated young people, not just in terms of basic literary skills, deciphering printed words or computing and analyzing numbers, but taking into account their ability to work cooperatively with others and to think creatively about challenges we cannot foresee. In her book lauding the wisdom of Peter Drucker, father of modern management, Elizabeth Edersheim (2007) highlights what schooling needs to become to help America compete in an emerging world economy:

> We have to retool our schools so that students don't simply learn how to answer multiple choice questions. They need to synthesize information and think critically. If we want our children to thrive in this new world, we should immerse them in Mandarin and other languages by the age of five so they learn to connect to other cultures and languages. (p. 38)

Many Native American tribes make important decisions by looking backward across four generations and forecasting three generations ahead. In education, we seem to be doing neither. We have little reverence for the past and cannot think beyond the concrete challenges we face day to day. If we consider where we have been and anticipate what lies ahead, we need to move beyond the constricted focus of current reform and contour our schools to meet the challenges of tomorrow as well as those close at hand.

NEW DIRECTIONS FOR NCLB's INTENTIONS

There are some provocative signposts sprinkled across miscellaneous current issues that point to a more promising strategic route to pull off NLCB's original goals and primary intent. The first clue appears in the formal commission's report analysis of what went wrong on or before September 11 that allowed nineteen terrorists to alter dramatically our way of life. One of the most important findings cited, but often overlooked, was the failure of imagination. The commission found it "crucial to finding a way of routinizing, even bureaucratizing, the exercise of imagination" (*The 9/11 Commission Report*, 2004, p. 344). There was a wealth of information containing clues that such an attack was possible, if not imminent. What was lacking was the mind's eye to piece the clues and signals together and to interpret what they meant. This void was also evident on the ground level where important day-to-day decisions are made. Immigration and Naturalization Service officers had several opportunities to deny most of the terrorists entry into the country. But they were going by the numbers and adhering strictly to protocol. Only one terrorist was stopped and denied access by an INS officer who relied on his intuition to make the decision.

The second interesting signpost that something new may be afoot to wean us from our infatuation with standardization, facts, and figures comes from California's university system. Often a harbinger of things to come, a systemwide university committee has issued a report recommending changes in admission requirements. Until now, students have been judged primarily by the numbers: grades and scores on the SAT or ACT tests. These tests, measuring verbal and quantitative aptitude, weigh especially heavily in admission decisions. Colleges and universities are ranked on aggregated test scores of entering freshmen. In this sense, the current emphasis on reading, writing, and numerical test results dovetails nicely with college admission standards.

The committee reached a different conclusion about admission standards. It concluded that grades and scores were not as important as "spark." This quality, the committee members agreed, was a better predictor of success in higher education than statistical assessments. "Spark" is not easy to quantify, but it's probably a complex blend of spunk, creative thinking, character, and enthusiasm. It's one of those qualities that's hard to pin down, yet easy to recognize. Its absence is also discernable at a deeper level of conjecture. University presidents are also rebelling against a ranking system that reduces the worth of their institution to a single mathematical score. Their argument:

> The rankings' formula overemphasizes selective admissions data like low acceptance rates and high SAT scores for incoming freshmen while giving short shrift to what really matters but is much harder to measure: the education students receive once they get on campus . . . few colleges, no matter how well endowed, are willing to risk their prestige by dropping out of what has become a hugely influential beauty contest. (Del Vecchio, 2007, pp. 49–50)

A final optimistic sign comes from the academic community. Alfie Kohn, for example, has leveled a continuous barrage of criticism at standardized tests and what they do or do not measure:

> What have the results of high-stakes testing been to this point? To the best of my knowledge, no positive effects have ever been demonstrated, unless you count higher scores on the same tests. More low-income students are dropping out, more teachers (often the best ones) are leaving the profession, and more mind-numbing test preparation is displacing genuine instruction. (Meier & Wood, 2004, p. 86)

Nel Noddings (2007) published an article in a national education magazine titled "The New Anti-Intellectualism in America." In it, she criticizes highly-structured, objective-focused, detailed instruction that "facilitates quick, shallow learning and swift forgetting." She elaborates in the following:

> *Students do not come to us as standard raw material, and we should not expect to produce standardized academic products. Intellectual life is challenging, enormously diverse, and rewarding. It requires initiative and independent thinking, not the tedious following of orders. It should not be reduced to mental drudgery. (p. 32)*

Weaving these clues and signs together, and reading between the strands, we catch a glimpse of the fundamental purpose of education far a field from the overemphasis of standards and testing. Reading, writing, and computation skills still matter, but imagination, intuition, spark, and independent thinking are the critical components of a well-educated person. As implemented, these are the very qualities so-called improvement efforts often stifle, routinize, or extinguish.

THREATS TO GLOBAL ADVANTAGE

This is precisely why our way of life is imperiled. America has historically been a country of inventors and entrepreneurs. Despite some obvious blemishes, this has created a place of opportunity and guaranteed a decent standard of living for many people. This is also America's comparative advantage in the global economy. The Japanese, for example, can perfect anything. If you want the world's finest croissant, go to Japan rather than Paris. But, in general, the Japanese are not inventors. In fact, they often send teams to figure out how America can produce such creative thinkers. If we continue on the present rational course, we put our most admirable virtues at risk.

That is why we need to take another tack. Put back into the hands of teachers and other leaders the responsibility to nourish imagination, intuition, and spark. Schools that strike a balance between vigor as well as rigor will create a learning environment that prevents dropouts and assures that students who don't fit a predetermined mold will not be left behind. Restoring the magic and soul of teaching and learning is our primary challenge. As Carl Cohn (2007), well-seasoned Superintendent of Schools in San Diego, observes:

> In my lifetime, I have experienced the large-scale application of so many theories of school reform. Each of these theories—from class-size reduction to whole language reading instruction—has failed to live up to the expectations of the reformers. In some cases they have caused extensive harm. A lesson of these failures is that there are no quick fixes or perfect educational theories . . . . I believe there is a place where no child is left behind, where all children achieve grade-level proficiency and there is no achievement gap. It is called heaven . . . . It is even more unlikely to be achieved when this earth for many children living in our urban neighborhoods is far closer to hell . . . . School reform is a slow, steady, labor-intensive process. It is heavily dependent on harnessing the talents of individuals such as Erin Gruwell, the Long Beach teacher currently portrayed in the movie Freedom Writers, for transforming the lives of at-risk students rather than punishing them for noncompliance with bureaucratic mandates and destroying their initiative . . . [reform] success is dependant on empowering those at the bottom not punishing them from the top. (http://www.edweek.org/ew/article/2007/04/25/34cohn.h26html)

America, at the present moment, seems caught up in tackling problems from the apex of the government. Local problem? Look to state or federal officials to fix it. That is the route school reformers have taken as far back as memory will go. Problems quickly rise to the top for solutions, bypassing local ingenuity and creativity.

Compare that to some European cities' 2007 response to global warming. While highly visible legislators and policymakers trumpet the problem and argue about what to do, the locals are rolling up their sleeves and doing something. Initiatives from the local level are influencing national policies rather the other way around. For example, the small Swedish city of Vaxjo has reduced its CO_2 emissions by thirty percent since 1993. One of the city's residents commented, "People used to ask: isn't it better to do this at a national or international level? We want to show everyone else that you can accomplish a lot at the local level" (Ritter, 2007, p. A5). Maybe school reformers and local schools here have something to learn from our friends across the Atlantic.

SOME NEW WRINKLES

How will a different approach take shape and come to pass? One of the first requirements is treating education as a total community responsibility. Teachers mention the role of parents in their critique of reforms. But the local net of accountability must be cast even wider. Hillary Clinton is right on target when she writes that "it takes a village" to educate young people. In many places the notion of a village has given way to splintered special interest groups, each with its own agenda.

Bringing a community together around the purposes of education and then providing innovative ways to document how they're working is an essential first step. The village buy-in must include parents, community members, business partners, teachers, administrators, students, and politicians. This communal spirit and responsibility is not impossible to achieve in America, but it will require some hard work and skillful maneuvering on the part of community leaders from all sectors. As Jim Hager, a recent nominee for National School Superintendent of the Year put it,

Since the current villagers have no sense of village, today's [edu-cators] must use rituals, stories, ceremonies, and other symbols to transform a splintered culture into a common community based on shared educational values. (Bolman & Deal, 2006, p. 4)

Students profit from community applause for significant deeds. When a society takes its role in bringing up the young seriously, wonderful things can happen. The role of the community of Paso Robles, California, in paving the way for Jesus Solorio's appearance on television's *So You Think You Can Dance* is a dazzling example. Jesus grew up in Oak Park, a Paso Robles housing project. The possibility that he would join a gang and end up either in jail or dead by age twenty was very likely. But the city and housing authority had cooperated to create an afterschool recreation program and Jesus enrolled in a dance class. From the get-go it was obvious that he had real talent. Members of the community chipped in to pay for advanced lessons at a local studio. His rhythm and movement progressed to the point that he was discovered by a professional dancer with an eye for flair. This opened the door to the big time: "Jesus danced through it. And then we all saw the result of a caring community—the rising young star on national television" (George, 2007, p. B5). Stories like this can't help but rally communities to give their young people a boost. They won't all make national television appearances, but, properly nudged and supported, all students can find their niche. Teachers welcome all the help they can muster. Whatever void they cannot fill, a community can take up the slack.

Our society also believes that for every problem someone has to be to blame. Schools, parents, teachers, or students invariably are faulted for education's shortcomings. But it is important to remember that when you point the finger of blame, three fingers point back your way. In Denmark, for example, the blame game doesn't exist. The entire community takes responsibility for assuring that all young people have the basics necessary for a productive, independent life:

Only when these prerequisites are in place can there be a mean-ingful discussion of the role of schools in making sure that no children are left behind. Talk about accountability is empty talk when its focus is exclusively on the individual and never on the society. (Morrill, 2007, p. 34)

A second approach is to encourage all people to reexamine the role teachers have played in their lives. Too often they either forget or keep it to themselves. As a result, teachers never fully reap the benefits of the seeds they've sown. Years ago, Peabody College of Vanderbilt University created a novel way to honor teachers. The award capitalized on one of the most widely rec-ognized symbols of teaching—the apple. Peabody put a mod-ern twist on the ancient ritual with a crystal apple. Anyone who donated a certain amount of money to the school was given the privilege of honoring a significant teacher. From a small begin-ning, the Crystal Apple Awards Night expanded into a com-munity-wide event. Nashville's mayor, politicians, businesspeople, and other notables attended. At its zenith, the celebration attracted well over a thousand people. Honorees accompanied their sponsors and their pictures flashed on a large screen throughout a catered dinner. Each was awarded a beautiful crystal apple. It was a fitting tribute to the community of teachers past and present. Nashville's awareness of the spe-cial contribution of teachers was accentuated.

The in-vogue bandwagon of standards and accountability stresses the shortcomings of schools and places a high pre-mium on things that may not matter that much in the larger picture. It seems foolhardy to think about a parent slapping his or her child each morning, telling them how poorly they're doing, and sending them off to school. But that's akin to what we do to teachers today. If we treat teachers well and give them support rather than condemnation, we might find that's the way they turn out. Saying "thank you" to teachers who have contributed something to each of us would go a long way in improving their morale and willingness to keep the faith.

A friend of ours received a telephone call recently. He's retired from active teaching and has been plagued with the all-too-familiar pathologies of aging. The call was from one of his former students. She had called information in nearly every area code in California trying to chase him down. She just wanted to tell him how much his high school history class had meant to her. If our friend ever had any doubts about the impact of his classroom career, they vanished at that moment. One short telephone conversation did the trick. The call even helped him put his health problems in perspective.

His is not an isolated case. A similar story was reported recently in the San Luis Obispo newspaper:

> *Jim, a local veteran elementary school teacher, was reading his e-mails and opened one that surprised him. A former student searched for "Mr. Howe favorite teacher" on Google and found him! The student's message was simple: He wanted to offer his deepest thanks for the positive impact Mr. Howe had made on his life as a third grader thirty-four years ago.* (George, 2007, p. B5)

In the December 12, 2007 issue of *BusinessWeek*, Robert Pondiscio, former communications director for the magazine, wrote about his experience as a teacher. He left a high-paying position to teach students in one of New York City's public schools. His first five years were rewarding, but then his experience soured. He had trouble with both students and parents and ultimately decided to quit. The key question was what to do next. In the process of looking for another job, he received a call from a mother of one of his former students. This student had been high performing and he had encouraged her to apply for an opportunity to be groomed for a place in a school that catered to very talented young people. The mother called to inform him that the student had been accepted and let him know that he had made a real difference: "I realized that I had dramatically changed the life of at least one terrific kid. It was the single greatest moment in my professional life." (p. SC05)

These anecdotes are just a small tip of a huge iceberg of privately held sentiments. Given the chance, millions of people would credit teachers for an encounter that channeled their life in a new direction. Leonard Pellicer, in the Foreword, talks about his seminars at locations across the country. At the beginning of his presentation he asks audiences to think about their "Personal Board of Directors," people who have had a positive influence on their lives. He then asks for a show hands for particular categories. One or two hands go up for doctors, engineers, business executives, or attorneys. The he asks about teachers on their personal list. All the hands go up. Two teachers? Hands still rose. He often goes as high as six or seven teachers with a few hands still up.

But few, if any, of those teachers who made such a profound impact will ever realize the tremendous good they have done. Instead, they will continue to receive the generalized wrath of policymakers and the public aimed at an amorphous mass of educators who are labeled as laggards unable to make a dent on short-term indicators of questionable validity. Of course, there are teachers who have died on the vine and continued to draw a salary. But any enterprise has its share of poisonous people who try to conscript others into their negative realm. Those malcontents should not command our attention, as they too often do. Another approach seems more promising. How can we now begin to recognize those tireless teachers whose long-term influence continues to shape young lives?

SIMPLE THINGS MEAN A LOT

In this book, we have provided examples of how special events might be organized and executed to honor teachers. It can be as simple as opening the school year with former students returning to let teachers know how much they have contributed to their lives. A school board meeting devoted to honoring teachers should be a yearly, if not monthly, occasion.

School boards are typically singled out for dysfunction, but the fact is, board members often do not understand their symbolic value in extolling the virtues of good teachers. In recognizing hopeful exemplars, we promote positive role models for others to emulate.

There is a more technologically driven possibility to consider. If an energetic student can track down a teacher whose past efforts mattered so much, why can't we take advantage of the Internet to systemize the connections? If the miracle of technology can link buyers with sellers, graduates with former school chums, and soul-searchers with soul mates, how about a network channel to give people a handy opportunity to thank a former teacher. The fact that there are so many with such gratitude to express might help refocus national attention on the real purpose of education. It would make a lot of aging teachers proud of what they have accomplished and maybe help others believe they might too.

Aside from recognizing individual teachers, another promising avenue for instilling pride in the teaching profession involves taking a closer look at the quality of organizations where teachers do their important work. As Hagar suggested above, paying more attention to the culture of schools could go a long way in improving education. Presently culture receives short shrift. It is eclipsed by the focus on rationality rather than spirituality. Someone has to take a leading role in infusing the school with meaning. Very often the person taking charge will be a teacher who serves the role of informal priest or priestess, or a teacher who is a recognized storyteller. They will help convene the special occasions that give a school good spirits and gusto. In individual classrooms, teachers play a key role in developing a shared sense of community, but teachers also need to recognize that a school has effects above and beyond the self-contained classroom. Working in a toxic or sterile environment deadens the heart and soul. Teachers know how to make it more meaningful. They simply need to expand their talent for creating a healthy, effervescent classroom to include their schools, their districts, and even the wider educational community.

REVIVING THE MAGIC

Will this spiritual transformation happen? It all depends. If past is prologue, we're doomed to continue toward the goal of trying to make schools more rational and accountable. We have been on that course for a long time, even though our efforts are redundant and our progress is puny. Businesses are gradually waking up to see that reaping profits requires attending to the soft, human aspects of what motivates people to put their hearts as well as their hands to work. In education this will not require a giant step forward but a lingering glance to the past. Teaching was once a calling. You didn't become a teacher to make a fortune; you became a teacher to make a difference. The purpose of your profession wasn't to convey information to be quickly forgotten, but to alter the course of a young person's life forever. You knew deep down that you couldn't do it for everyone. You hoped you could do it for a few. That flickering hope was enough to help you keep the devotion burning when the going got tough.

Somewhere along the line, we've lost touch with a hallowed conception of teaching. But as someone once said, "No one can take your spirit from you. You have to give it away. But you can always take it back." Now is the time to emerge from our rationalist stupor and reclaim the stature and glory of an essential role in the cultivation and perpetuation of our way of life. We cannot afford the alternative. Our offspring and their dedicated mentors deserve better. There is no reason why they can't experience the best—with some hard work on the right things.

Now is the time for educators to reawaken and reassert the heart and soul of education. Many educators clamor for a recipe for how this can be done. There is none. New approaches to persisting problems will be honed by people willing to look inside themselves, identify their passion, and find a way to join others in a virtuous quest to reshape education in positive ways. Will they succeed? Who knows? Will they fail? Probably once in awhile. Either way they may leave a legacy that will linger. That's what leadership's all about. And that's what we need to restore more heft to the spiritual facet of education and bring it into parity with the technical. This does not imply retreating from standards and testing. It means redirecting time and attention to the values, traditions, and essence of institutions and individuals that mold young people and perpetuate our way of life. At present, things are dangerously out of whack. To correct the imbalance, we need to throw more weight on the symbolic end of the teeter-totter. This sentiment is best summed up by an ad on the New York subway: "You remember your first-grade teacher's name. Who will remember yours?"

Remembrance works both ways. A teacher writes, "At the end of the teaching day I leave the classroom but I am still, and shall ever be a teacher. Time ago I was that child for whom such commitment made a difference. I will dedicate my days confident my efforts matter . . . because of one child." (Goldberg & Feldman, 2003, pg. 2)

How these efforts matter to each of us is echoed by another teacher. "Just think about what you know today. You read. You write. You work with numbers. You solve problems. We take all these things for granted. But of course you haven't always read. You haven't always known how to write. You weren't born knowing how to subtract 199 from 600. Someone showed you. There was a moment when you moved from not knowing to knowing, from not understanding to understanding. *That's* why I became a teacher." (Done, 2005).

References

Allison, M. (2004, February 24). Starbucks must find "lost" soul. *Seattle Times.* Retrieved October, 18, 2007, from http://Seattle Times.nwsource.com/html/businesstechnology/2003586922 starbucks24.html

Ayers, W. (2001). *To teach: The journey of a teacher.* New York: Teachers College Press.

Barth, R. (2001). *Learning by heart.* San Francisco: Jossey-Bass.

Bell, C. (2005). It takes a teacher. *Life Magazine,* p.8.

Bolman, L., & Deal, T. (2003). *Reframing organizations.* San Francisco: Jossey-Bass.

Bolman, L., & Deal, T. (2005). *The wizard and the warrior.* San Francisco: Jossey-Bass.

Bullough. R. V. (2006, November). Developing interdisciplinary researchers: Whatever happened to the humanities in education. *Educational Researcher,* p. 8.

Clinton, H. (2006). *It takes a village.* New York: Simon & Schuster.

Cohn, C. (2007, April 25). Empowering those at the bottom beats punishing them from the top. Retrieved 6/12/07, from http://www.edweek.org/ew/articles/2007/04/25/34cohn

Cuban, L. (1993). *How teachers taught.* New York: Teachers College Press.

Cuban, L. (2004). *The blackboard and the bottom line.* Cambridge, MA: Harvard University Press.

Cubberly, E. (1916). *Public school administration.* Boston: Houghton Mifflin.

Deal, T., & Nolan, R. (1978). *Alternative schools.* Chicago: Nelson Hall.

Del Vecchio, R. (2007, September 9). Reports calls UC's admissions unfair. *The San Francisco Chronicle,* pp. 49–50.

Deming, W. (1986). *Out of the crisis.* New York: Dell.

DePree, Max. *Leadership is an Art.* New York: Dell, 1989.

Done, P. (2005). 32 *Third graders and one class bunny: life lessons from teaching.* New York, NY: Touchstone, Simon & Shuster.

Edersheim, E. (2007). *The definitive Drucker.* New York: McGraw-Hill.

Ferris, R. (1999). The mechanics of learning. In E. Wright (Ed.), *Why I teach* (pp. 15–21). Roseville, CA: Prima Publishing.

Fox, M. (1995). *The reinvention of work.* New York: HarperOne.

George, B. (2007, July 20). Our children need us. *The San Luis Obispo Tribune*, p. B5.

Gerstner, L. (2002). *Who says elephants can't dance?* New York: HarperCollins.

Gill, N. G. (2007, July 17). Goodbye, Mr. and Ms. Chips. *Education Week*, p. 35.

Gladwell, M. (2002). *The tipping point.* New York: Bayback Books.

Goldberg, M. S. & Feldman, S. (2003). *Teachers with class.* Kansas City, MO: Andrews McMeel Publishing.

Gross, D. (2007, March 4). Starbucks' venti problem. *The Los Angeles Times*, p. M1.

Gruwell, E. (1999). *The freedom writers.* New York: Broadway Books.

Guralnik, D. (Ed.). (1986) *Webster's College Dictionary* (2nd ed.), p. 722. New York: Prentice Hall.

Heath, C., & Heath, D. (2007). *Made to stick.* New York: Random House.

Hindo, B. (2007, June 11). At 3M, a struggle between efficiency and creativity. *Business Week*, p. 10.

Hirschman, A. O. (1970). *Exit, voice and loyalty.* Cambridge, MA: Harvard University Press.

Kidder, T. (1989). *Among schoolchildren.* Boston: Houghton Mifflin.

Ladson-Billings, G. (1994). *The dream keepers.* San Francisco: Jossey-Bass.

Lopez, B., & Pohrt, L. (1998). *Crow and weasel.* New York: Farrar, Strau, & Giroux.

McCourt, F. (2005). *Teacher man.* New York: Scribner.

Meier, D., & Wood, G. (2004). *Many children left behind.* Boston: Beacon Press.

Meyer, J., & Rowan, B. (1978). The structure of education organizations. In M.W. Meyer (Ed.), *Environments in organizations* (pp. 78–109). San Francisco: Jossey-Bass.

Morrill, R. (2007, April 11). Monopoly and "No Child Left Behind." *Education Week*, p. 34.

Noddings, N. (2007, March 21). The new anti-intellectualism in America. *Education Week*, pp. 31–32.

Palmer, P. (1998). *The courage to teach.* San Francisco: Jossey-Bass.

Pondiscio, R. (2007, December 17). "'Mr. P' Learns His Lesson. *Business Week*, pp. SC02–SC04.

Perlstein, L. (2007). *Tested*. New York: Henry Holt.

Ritter, K. (2007, October 15). To save the earth, European cities act locally. *San Luis Obispo Tribune*, p. A5.

Rosenthal, R., & Jacobson, L. (1968). *Pygmalion in the classroom*. New York: Holt, Rinehart & Winston.

Russo, A.(Producer), & Hiller, A. (Director). (1984). *Teachers* [Motion picture]. United States: MGM/Universal Artists.

Schultz, H. (1997). *Pour your heart into it*. New York: Hyperion.

Tyack, D., & Cuban, L. (1995). *Tinkering toward utopia*. Cambridge, MA: Harvard University Press.

Tyack, D., & Hansot, E. (1982). *Managers of virtue*. New York: Basic Books.

Waller, W. (1932). *The sociology of teaching*. New York: John Wiley & Sons.

Weeks, J. (2003). *One big fat fig: All together now*. Chicago: Houghton Mifflin.

Wolcott, H. (2003). *Teachers vs. technocrats*. Eugene, OR: Altamira Press.

Index

CORWIN PRESS

The Corwin Press logo—a raven striding across an open book—represents the union of courage and learning. Corwin Press is committed to improving education for all learners by publishing books and other professional development resources for those serving the field of PreK–12 education. By providing practical, hands-on materials, Corwin Press continues to carry out the promise of its motto: **"Helping Educators Do Their Work Better."**

NSDC's purpose: Every educator engages in effective professional learning every day so every student achieves.